CRYPTOCURRENCY FOR BEGINNERS

A Guide To Grow Your Financial Future in 2021 by Investing in Bitcoin, Eth, Ltc, Xrp and Others

Written By: Robert J. Morales

1

2

INTRODUCTION

Cryptocurrencies use a number of terms in the common analog-age lexicon. From the term 'coin' to the term 'blockchains,' to even the concept of 'payment' and 'ownership,' and seemingly unrelated terms like 'mining'. I will tell you here and now, none of these terms are used in the way they used to mean, and you will see why in just a moment. I will show you what they really mean and put you on the path to understanding how to trade these coins, and what instruments you can use to approach this market with competence and confidence. I will also show you how to look for opportunities and even use algorithms to trade rapidly, instead of manually clicking the buy or sell button, or manually drawing lines and charts to anticipate movements.

Why would you want to trade cryptocurrencies? It's not because it is the latest craze, but because it is the latest money-making potential that rivals the early days of Wall Street, and the Forex market. It is a market that naturally lends itself to electronic trades, and thereby makes entry and exit fluid and efficient. Can you lose money on this? Sure you can. Nothing is guaranteed and, in fact, not only is it not guaranteed, the chances of you losing money trading cryptos is very high if you do not know what you are doing.

WHAT IS CRYPTOCURRENCY ?

Cryptocurrency is an online mechanism of exchange that uses cryptographic functions to execute cash transactions. Cryptocurrencies use the technology of blockchain to improve immutability, accountability, and decentralization. The cryptocurrency's most significant characteristic is that it is not regulated by any centralized authority: the blockchain's decentralized nature makes cryptocurrency potentially free from the old ways of government control and intervention. Using private and public key you can transfer cryptocurrencies directly between the two parties. All such transfers can be made at minimal fees, which enables users to avoid high fees charged by traditional financial institutions. For a more suitable description, cryptocurrencies are essentially currencies that don't have a centralized issuer as the central bank of a country. These are generated using methods of computer encryption that restrict the quantity of money units (or coins) produced and then verify the transfer of funds after creation. Because of its theoretical similarity to gold mining or other precious metals this creation technique is known as "mining." You'll need to solve an increasingly complex algorithm or puzzle to mine cryptocurrency. Solving such algorithms requires a lot of computer processing power. In other words, mining them is costing money so we can not just create value from thin air. As a result, as opposed to any central government or bank, certain currencies and their interests are protected by mathematical rule.

As blockchain's popularity increases, so does the number of uses in the real world. With cryptocurrencies, you can purchase anything from physical goods, gift cards, sports tickets and even hotel bookings. Many bars and restaurants have also started accepting it as payment method. A number of charities now accept donations in Bitcoin, and also other tokens. In the case of underground online markets dealing with illegal goods such as Silk Road and Alpha Bay there are also more illicit examples. These currencies have enormous advantages over the currencies we know and are using today. This is what makes them so appealing to both long-term buyers and short-term speculators. As with any kind of investment, of course.

After 1998 the notion of' cryptocurrencies' has been at the debate itself. B-Money and Bit Gold were the first known attempt to create a digital cryptocurrency but both never came into existence. Cryptocurrencies are the digital or virtual currencies which operate on the principles of cryptography. As the name suggests, it has no physical existence, and it is not measurable. They exist merely as a set of programming codes. Yet it provides high security and flexibility compared with many currencies in existence.

Cryptocurrency operates on blockchain technology, and we have seen how blockchain works already. In cryptocurrency, the ledger retains the track of cryptocurrency developed and transacted across the network. In a specific blockchain each user will have a unique account ID / address. The coin is always linked with this account (Currency is debited and given credit towards that account). The so called wallets program helps people to manage their money. Through the wallets, anyone can make the transaction to someone on the network (both the sender and the receiver must have an account). The transfers are checked by nodes and added to the blockchain ledger.So blockchain's immutable and encrypted ledger is cryptocurrency's backbone. When you completely eliminate and simplify to a basic definition all the complexity surrounding cryptocurrencies, you may find that a database comprises only a few submissions that nobody can alter without having met specific conditions. It may sound odd but believe it or not: this is precisely how to characterize a currency.

Keep the money into your banking account: what is more than a record entry that only under specific conditions can be changed? It is even possible to take notes & physical coins: what are something other than minimal entries in a physical general database which can only be switched if you suit the condition when physically owning the coins and notes? Money is all about a verified entry into some type of account, balance, and transaction database.

A formal definition–Cryptocurrency is an Internet based system that uses cryptographic functions to exchange financial transactions. Cryptocurrencies leverages blockchain technology to improve decentralisation, transparency and immutability.

A BRIEF HISTORY OF CRYPTOCURRENCY

While the practical applications of cryptocurrencies date back a mere 7 years, the technical aspects actually date back a further 30 years to the 1980s. Cryptographer David Chaum was the first to theorize a cryptocurrency when he invented an encrypted computer algorithm that allowed secure, unalterable exchanges between two parties. Chaum later founded DigiCash, among the first enterprises to produce currency units based on his algorithm. It is important to note that the currency, which is a model unlike Bitcoin and other cryptocurrencies in which anyone can mine the currency (providing they have the necessary computing power), could only be produced by the DigiCash firm. The company went bankrupt in the late 1990s after getting into legal problems and rejecting a deal with Microsoft that would have seen DigiCash bundled with every home Windows operating system.

Chinese software engineer Wei Dai published a white paper on "b-money", which laid the foundations for the architecture behind the cryptocurrencies that we know today. The paper included information on complex algorithms, anonymity for purchasers and decentralization. However the currency itself never came to fruition. US based E-Gold was another failed attempt at creating a cryptocurrency in the 1990s. The Florida based company gave customers e-gold "tokens" in exchange for their jewelry, old trinkets and coins. These tokens could then be exchanged for US dollars. The website was initially successful and there were over 1 million active accounts by the mid-2000s. One of E-Gold's pioneering strategies was that anyone could open an account. However, this led to a number of scams being run through the website. In addition, poor security protocols led to large hacking incidents and the company went out of business in 2009.

The modern cryptocurrencies that we know today began with Bitcoin, which was first outlined by anonymous entity (the identity has never been confirmed as a single person or group) Satoshi Nakamoto. Bitcoin was released to the public in early 2009 and a large group of enthusiasts began mining, investing in, and exchanging the currency. The first Bitcoin market was established in February 2010. In late 2012 Hosting and website development platform Wordpress became the first major retailer to support payment in Bitcoin. This step was key as it gave the currency real world credibility and showed that large corporations had confidence in it as a currency.

COMPARING CRYPTOCURRENCY WITH TRADITIONAL CURRENCY

Any currency's value is based by what someone gives you in exchange for said currency. Currencies, cryptography or otherwise must respect three basic rules:

- They need to be difficult to produce (cash) or find (gold or other precious metals)
- They need have a limited supply
- They need to be recognized by other humans as having value

Using only Bitcoin (BTC) as an example, it ticks the boxes of all three of these characteristics:

- Bitcoin uses complex computer algorithms in its production which take a lot of computational power, so it cannot be replicated easily or at a discount
- Bitcoins come in a finite supply – twenty one Million to be exact. As of 2015, roughly 2/3 of this number had been mined
- There are hundreds of Bitcoin exchanges and Bitcoin is accepted everywhere from Subway to OKCupid

Where cryptocurrencies differ from traditional currencies (also known as Fiat currencies) is that they are not tied to any one country, nation or institution (in most cases). There are no USA Bitcoins, no Japanese Litecoins or anything like that. They are decentralized. Bitcoin was designed as a "deflationary currency" - meaning over time its value will, in theory, inherently increase. Unlike fiat currencies which are inflationary and whose value will eventually decrease. After all, in 1917, $1 was worth the equivalent of $20.17 today. So the US Dollar is worth 20 times LESS than 100 years ago. In other words, if you continue to hold $1 over the course of 100 years, you will be able to buy progressively fewer and fewer items in exchange for it, whereas with Bitcoin, the opposite will happen. As another real world example. On 22 May 2010, Laszlo Hanyecz made the first real-world cryptocurrency transaction by buying two pizzas in Jacksonville, Florida for 10,000 BTC. Today 10,000BTC is worth over $101 million. Bitcoin was designed this way so that no single person (or government) could increase the supply of money, lowering the value of the money already in the market.

We also have to remember that fiat currencies that we know and love were not always the main players in the currency world. For centuries, Gold and other precious metals were seen as the most desirable currencies for day to day usage. It was not until governments could standardize and verify the metallic content of coins (and later paper bills) that they became the go to choice for citizens.

While Bitcoin has an air of uncertainty about it based on the decentralization principle - where the real potential lies is in seeing it from the opposite perspective. With no single body being responsible for the supply of money, it forces all players (government, businesses and consumers) to be transparent about their processes, lowering the risk of fraud or tampering. The transparency is ensured by rewarding miners for their efforts (in the form of coin). This single dominating factor is why so many investors are confident about the long term viability of the currency.

One common argument made by Bitcoin detractors is that as there is no government backing the currency, it could totally collapse in theory. However, we have seen these happen numerous times with fiat currency under scenarios of hyperinflation where governments can no longer ensure the value of their money and as such have to create an entirely new currency. Common examples include the German Weimar Republic in the 1920s, where the currency lost so much of its value, banknotes were used as wallpaper. Currently, the Venezuelan economy is on track to experience over 1000% inflation for the year, leaving many citizens unable to afford daily necessities like bread. Bitcoin enthusiasts see the cryptocurrency as recession-proof. The cost of international transactions is another area where cryptocurrencies maintain a huge advantage over traditional ones. Anyone who has ever had to send money overseas will know that the cost of processing these transaction can reach ridiculous levels. There are times when these fees can top 10%. As cryptocurrencies do not view international transactions (as there are no "nations" involved) any differently from local ones, there are minimal fees for sending money to any part of the world. The speed of transactions across borders is also much faster than regular fiat currencies, a Bitcoin transaction takes around 10 minutes to register as opposed to days for international bank transfers, and other coins process transactions even faster.

UNDERSTANDING BLOCKCHAIN TECHNOLOGY

So how is all that money worth anything at all? The solution to this is blockchain tech. If you intend to invest any money in cryptocurrencies at all, it is important that you have at least a basic understanding of blockchain technology and its applications. Blockchain technology allows a complete, incorruptible archive of all transactions that have ever existed, free of human errors or lack of evidence. The important thing to remember is that these transactions don't always have to be financial, they can be in the form of legal contracts, consumer goods audits and file storage. Blockchain is basically a giant database not stored at a central location. If you like, A floating folder. The transactions documented on the blockchain are publicly accessible and verifiable because it is not held in any single location. We are returning to the idea of decentralization again, and not having to rely on a single person or government to make sure our transactions are secure.

Imagine all of the financial information stored on a single spreadsheet in more practical terms, not particularly safe right? Even if you had online and offline copies, there would only be 2 to 3 failure points. What blockchain allows is that spreadsheet to be distributed across thousands of databases and continuously refreshed meaning any changes will be recorded and no hacker could corrupt it at a single entry point. Since there is no single entry point, there is no single fault point either as well. Blockchain technology could be used to move everything from bitcoin to tangible assets like land, without needing to use a middle man like a bank or other financial institution. This has potential to save trillions of dollars a year that are wasted on transaction fees for consumers and businesses.

Although Bitcoin has attracted more consumer-related mainstream press, the blockchain technology is getting further business interest. Blockchain is an irrefutably resourceful invention which is bringing about a revolution in the global business market. Its evolution has brought with it a greater good, not only for businesses but for its beneficiaries as well. But since its revelation to the world, a vision of its operational activities is still unclear. The main question that sticks in everyone's mind is - What is Blockchain?

To start with, Blockchain technology serves as a platform that allows the transit of digital information without the risk of being copied. It has, in a way, laid the foundation of a strong backbone of a new kind of internet space. Originally designed to deal with Bitcoin - trying to explain to the layman about the functions of its algorithms, the hash functions, and digital signature property, today, technology buffs are finding other potential uses of this immaculate invention which could pave the way to the onset of an entirely new business dealing process in the world. Blockchain, to define in all respects, is a kind of algorithm and data distribution structure for the management of electronic cash without the intervention of any centralized administration, programmed to record all the financial transactions as well as everything that holds value.

THE WORKING OF BLOCKCHAIN

Blockchain can be comprehended as Distributed Ledger technology which was originally devised to support the Bitcoin cryptocurrency. But post heavy criticism and rejection, the technology was revised for use in more productive things. To give a clear picture, imagine a spreadsheet that's practically augmented across a plethora of computing systems. And then imagine that these networks are designed to update this spreadsheet from time to time. This is exactly what blockchain is. Information that's stored on a blockchain is a shared sheet whose data is reconciled from time to time. It's a practical way that speaks of many obvious benefits. To being with, the blockchain data doesn't exist in one single place. This means that everything stored in there is open for public view and verification. Further, there isn't any centralized information storing platform which hackers can corrupt. It's practically accessed over a million computing systems side-by-side, and its data can be consulted by any individual with an internet connection.

Blockchain technology is something that mimics the internet space. It's robust in nature. Similar to offering data to the general public through the World Wide Web, blocks of authentic information are stored on blockchain platforms which are identically visible on all networks.

Vital to note, blockchain cannot be controlled by a single person, entity or identity, and has no one point of failure. Just like the internet has proven itself as a durable space for the last 30 years, blockchain too will serve as an authentic, reliable global stage for the business transaction as it continues to develop.

USERS OF BLOCKCHAIN

There isn't a defined rule or regulation about who shall or can make use of this technology. Though at present, its potential users are banks, commercial giants and global economies only. The technology is open for the day to day transactions of the general public as well. The only drawback blockchain is facing is global acceptance.

HOW DOES BLOCKCHAIN RELATE TO BITCOIN AND CRYPTOCURRENCY?

Did you know the Blockchain is not the same thing as Bitcoin? If you used the terms interchangeably, you're not alone; lots of people are doing the same thing, mostly because blockchain and bitcoin are so closely connected. If you've ever scratched your head wondering what the difference between the two is on earth, then this article is for you. In super-simple terms a blockchain is a data storage computer file. And, to put it in more technical jargon, it's a transparent, distributed ledger (database), ensuring the data contained within the blockchain is distributed (duplicated) across many machines and is therefore decentralized.

This decentralisation is one of the things which makes blockchain so revolutry. In comparison to a conventional, centralized database–where documents are handled by one central administrator (say, a corporation or government)–the whole blockchain is open, and user consent verifies the data. But blockchains remain incredibly secure given the secrecy. That's because hackers don't have to hit one specific point of attack. You're on target! Blockchain is the technology underpinning Bitcoin, and it was specifically developed for Bitcoin. Yeah, Bitcoin was the first proof of blockchain in practice and there wouldn't be a Bitcoin without blockchain. Therefore the two names are used interchangeably so often. But that doesn't mean the same thing for blockchain and bitcoin. Bitcoin is a distributed, decentralized currency or peer-to-peer electronic payment mechanism where users may anonymously pass bitcoins without intervention from third parties (such as a bank or government). Nevertheless, Bitcoin is just one example of a cryptocurrency; blockchain technology often powers other crypto-currency networks. So while Bitcoin uses digital currency exchange blockchain technology, blockchain is more than just a bitcoin. Since blockchain and bitcoin are so inextricably linked, it took a long time for people to realize that blockchain does have far broader uses than cryptocurrency networks. In reality, the promise of blockchain is so great that many people (including myself) claim the system can revolutionize the way we do business, just as before the internet did.

Here are just a few examples of broader blockchain implementations outside cryptocurrencies & bitcoin:

Carrying out smart contracts. Thanks to Bitcoin, we all know the blockchain is awesome to allow digital transactions but it can also be used through smart contracts to formalize digital relationships. Automated payments can be issued with a smart contract once the terms of the contract have been met and promises to save time and help minimize conflicts or resolve disputes.

• Maintain a common, open recording system; Blockchain is the ideal solution to create a long-term, safe and open database of properties that all parties can access safely (land rights would be a good example of that).

• Supply chain analysis. Blockchain lets users track ownership records for products all the way back to source. As an example of this, De Beers Diamond company has begun using blockchain to trace diamonds from the mine to the end customer. Everyone wanting to verify if their diamonds are conflict-free will have a clear and accurate record.

• Providing insurance certificates. Nationwide insurance company plans to use blockchain to provide insurance proof-of-information. The device will help police officers, insurers and consumers quickly check insurance coverage which should help speed up the claims process.

To summarize, let's remember that blockchain and bitcoin are two separate things: • Bitcoin is a cryptocurrency, whereas blockchain is a centralized ledger.

• Bitcoin is powered by blockchain technology but many uses have been found beyond Bitcoin.

• Bitcoin encourages anonymity and blockchain promotes transparency. Blockchain has to meet specific Know Your Customer rules to be applied in certain sectors (especially banking).

• Bitcoin exchanges money between it users while blockchain can be used to transfer any kinds of things, including property rights & information..

Btc is not blockchain and Bitcoin or any other crypto-currency is not bitcoin. Bitcoins or other tokens are transacted on a blockchain technology running on a public network.

Blockchain is the underlying technology that makes Bitcoin and other transactions in cryptocurrency, blockchain technology has many more potential uses. You may think of blockchain as an operating system, and of Bitcoin as one of the hundreds of applications running on it.

FUNDAMENTALS OF CRYPTOCURRENCIES

Cryptocurrency, or crypto for short, is an electronic form of currency that allows the transmission of value between two nodes on a network. There are two specific networks that you should get familiar with, because they are currently the most widely known and the ones with the most activity. Fair warning: that could change over time. But as long as you understand the basics, it doesn't matter what the branding is. The first network is the Bitcoin network and the second is the Ethereum network.

What do coins and currencies have to do with networks? Think of Bitcoin and Ethereum as two individual networks. Although they comprise of thousands of nodes and hundreds and thousands of users, the ecosystem is a closed loop. The coins never actually leave the network and that network is defined by the existence of nodes.

Nodes

Nodes are computers that are part of the network. To become a node, users download and install the relevant software. The software itself is free, and once installed it opens up a port on the host computer and automatically connects it to a number of other nodes within the network. Each node connects directly to any node in the network, usually only around six at a time. At the last count, there were almost 12,000 of these nodes and each node connects to six others. It may not seem like much, but if you wanted to send a message to the entire network, all you have to do is send it to the six you are connected to and they will relay it to the six each of them is connected to and those nodes will relay that message on, and within 5 to 6 hops, your message will have spread to all 12000 nodes. Why are messages important? Because the message is the root of the transaction. We will look at the transaction next.

Transaction

The transaction needs to have two elements to it to make it legitimate. First it needs witnesses, and second it needs a reason. A reason is typically, within the Bitcoin network, the movement of tokens from the sender to the receiver. The sender initiates a message on the network messaging system and sends it to the receiver's address. Imagine if I send you a letter saying that I will give you a dollar and everyone in this town is a witness to that. There is no way of reversing that transaction. The promise is irrevocable. The transaction in Ether or Bitcoin is as simple as that. To initiate a transaction, the sender must have the funds and he must send the message. When he has the funds and sends a message, so that all the nodes bear witness to it, that transaction is legitimized.

Transaction Value

The value of the transaction can be any amount. If it's Bitcoin, it can be as small as 100 millionth of one Bitcoin (0.00000001). That is the smallest value that the messaging system recognizes. It is also called 1 Satoshi (in honor of the person who developed the Bitcoin system). The largest amount is whatever amount you have in that wallet, and you can have as many wallets as you like.

Wallets

Wallets are not the kind that you place in your pocket. On the surface, the wallet is the mailbox that holds the coins that you receive in a message. When you send a message out as part of a transaction, it will come from this mailbox – specifically called an address. If that address (we called it mailbox here for recognition of concept) has previously received coins, then it has the ability to spend those coins. If it has no coins, that address will not be able to send out a transaction message.

A wallet is really an app installed on your device (computer or mobile device) that looks across all the transactions and finds out which transactions in the entire ledger relate to that address. All transactions are categorized as either incoming or outgoing. It adds up all the incoming transactions, and then it separately adds up all the outgoing transactions, and the difference results in your account balance – or the maximum amount that you can transact out.

The only other thing that you need to know is the difference between hot and cold wallets. Hot wallets are ones that are constantly connected to the Internet and accessible at any time. Cold Wallets on the other hand are ones that are not online and can't be accessed via the internet.

The Coin

It's hard to wrap one's mind around the concept of the coin, or the crypto coin as it is also known. The reason is psychological. We see it as a coin because coins represent tangible currency in our mind. It gives us a frame of reference as a vessel of value. When we mention a coin, it wraps our mind around a new concept using old and familiar vernacular. But the coin in the crypto economy is nothing like the coin we think of that is typically round and flat with engravings on both sides. In fact, all the images you see online that represent Bitcoin as a golden circular coin are merely imaginary. It does not look anything like that.

Some even think of the coin as a string of bits – ones and zeros of binary computer language. But it's not. There is no physical coin, and there is not an electric coin either. In fact the coin is not even cryptographic. I know that this goes against all you have heard, but hang in there, you will see what it is in a minute. What it really is, is a cryptographic intra-network messaging system that cannot be forged or hacked. The key to why it can't be forged or hacked is because it is based on a transparent and decentralized system that is encrypted – more on the encryption and security in the next section.

The coin merely represents an irrevocable act of paying a certain value that is mentioned in the message. And because this is a trustless system, that promise is instantly verified by the system, which knows if the address from where the message is being sent has enough value to be transmitted. It is that value that is described as a coin.

In essence, crypto coin trading is as efficient and pure as it gets, because you are trading our purchasing value. But because it is hard for most people, who are not deeply familiar with the inner workings of the system, the term 'coin' gives them a sense of comfort by referring them to the objectification of the value that is being transmitted.

For the promise to have value, it must have been derived from value. You cannot just take something and arbitrarily bestow value upon it. Before it can have market value or face value, it must first have some form of intrinsic value. Without that the value is untradeable.

You must understand this at the core of your foray into crypto-economics and cryptocurrency trading.

The intrinsic value the 'coin' gets is derived from the physical labor that is performed to bring that 'coin' into existence. Resources need to be spent, and effort needs to be applied in creating each 'coin,' and that is why it is referred to as mining. Just as precious metals need to be physically mined, cryptographic value needs to be created by the expense of computational resources and cryptographic processes, and this is done by mining. The next section will describe the mining process.

Essentially, then, coins are brought to life as a reward for the mining process, which requires the expense of resource and cannot be derived for free. It is the nature of the Bitcoin system. In Ethereum, the expense of bringing a coin into existence is done by the expense of resources as well, but they will be converting from the Evidence of Work model to the Proof of Stake model in the future, barring any unforeseen changes. Either way, a value of some sort needs to be applied.

Once the coin is received by the person who expends this effort, he has the ability to spend it any way he wants. He can even give it away for free or he can use it as consideration for any product or service, as long as the recipient is willing to accept it. But let's look at that carefully for a minute.

The person who receives it from the system is called the miner, and we will explain that next, but for now, just know that in return for his mining, the system gives him and only him a certain number of coins (remember that coins in this context is just a value with no physical features).

When he spends that coin, he can only do it within the network. Of course, he can purchase whatever he wants, as long as the person he is buying from is within the network and has a valid address to receive that payment.

So now that value expended during the mining can be exchanged for anything and it is done so by a message that forms the transaction.

When you trade, that is what you are trading. That is what is called a coin.

Mining

Mining is discussed in this book for two reasons. The first is that it gives you an opportunity to invest in Cryptocurrencies in the form of mining. Even though you are interested in trading, mining is a form of investment in cryptos that are worth thinking about because the cost of mining has only a few factor inputs: electricity to run the computers, purchase of the computers, and the software and whatever labor costs the miner needs to perform the tasks. The hardware costs are typically one-off (there are also replacement costs, because the processors can burn out and might need replacing). Once you acquire the coins in this way, you can then use them to trade. That's one way of doing it. But not everyone wants to get knee-deep in the process. For those folks, we advise just getting to the exchange and starting your trading from there.

We mentioned earlier that mining is the process that brings the coins to life. But now we are going to look closely at what that is. In the next section, we will talk about the blockchain and what it is, but for now, just know that it exists.

While mining efforts result in rewards in the form of coins, the actual mining is the process of computation. In other words, mining is just really a ring of millions of computations to solve a puzzle. The first one to solve that puzzle will be awarded the coin. Thus, the question here is: what is the puzzle?

Without going in too deep, the puzzle relates to hashing. Hashing is a branch of mathematical cryptography that uses a one-way function that is deterministic. That means if I took a word and hashed it, I would get an unpredictable sequence of characters that cannot be reverse engineered.

I could take this entire book and hash it and what I will get is a string of characters that look like this (this is the hash of the following sentence: The rise and fall of the

Roman-Empire):

5C94D7845A6A2163D39CA32A0D19122C6B95FA591C
F58636DBEBB475EDA4A160

That hash is so unbreakable that even if I were to change one letter, or even the capitalization of that letter, see how the entire hash changes. I will hash the same sentence but with a minor change: the rise and fall of the Roman Empire. In this case, if you notice, the first alphabet has been changed to a lowercase.

AFC44E6D243443A56A2D65357FA98EA61A6A5997B
D2975C4435B9A4BCCCFB763

Looking very different when you observe the two hashes. There's no way you can modularize it, even if you understood how hashed it was. Now remember, these are just the basic parts of hashing. If you want to know more, there are numerous books that you can get to understand the hashing and cryptographic process in deeper detail.

Back to mining.

Every time a transaction is completed (a message to send coin from one account to another is broadcast through the network) two things happen. The first, is the nodes that receive the broadcast check to see if it is a valid transaction – specifically they see if the sender has a sufficient balance. The second thing they do is confirm if the message is properly formatted and all the details are present. There are about 16 checks that the nodes execute, and if all is okay, they place the transaction in a queue. At this point the transfer of value is not yet confirmed.

There are hundreds of these messages on an hourly basis in the queue.

The next thing that happens is the miners pull all these transactions (they take the transaction IDs) and put them together and hash them. There is a specific way to hash them and it has to include a few things. It needs to include the TXIDs, the header, the hash of the last block, and one more item called a nonce.

This nonce is a random number, but this is where the puzzle that needs to be solved comes into play. If you take all the information that goes into the block and run the hash function, it will result in a specific string of characters – just as the sentence "The rise and fall of the Roman Empire" above did. Now look at the sentence again, and the corresponding hash for it: the rise and fall of the Roman Empire

AFC44E6D243443A56A2D65357FA98EA61A6A5997B D2975C4435B9A4BCCCFB763

The rule is that you can't change any part of the sentence, but you can add random characters after it. With that in mind, what if I told you that the puzzle was to find the hash that started with the character 0 (zero)? Since you can't reverse engineer the hash, you have to randomly keep trying with different strings of characters that you can append to the sentence to make the hash start with 0. It would look something like this:

the rise and fall of the Roman Empire 5134525

52CBF3DF5DFA63DA68F55AA5BC321F36597E53D96
001B5D1E14668DE79F444E7

This wouldn't work because the resulting hash didn't begin with 0 as the system required.

The next try:

the rise and fall of the Roman Empire 4749q0r58tj

423C9570BC80747EC346626C8049208DBA52753BA
303516817D9CFC6390D1D10

This didn't work either. But just to make the point, after a few hundred tries the random number that worked was this:

the rise and fall of the Roman Empire 090989897934

Which resulted in the hash as below:

0C3EE05D5788E2FD0DFE4D49AE6109A1AFE36523
F0D99ED6DC48A4ECF8681622

That hash satisfied the requirement, and as such, the puzzle is solved.

Once the puzzle is solved, the coins are awarded to the miner that solved the puzzle and all the transactions that were included are now said to be part of a block with a specific hash. That hash is part of the record, and can never be changed. If the block can't be altered (because if you alter the block, the hash would change, and the system would know that there was a problem and reject that block) then the transactions within it can't be altered, either.

Once that block is confirmed, all the transactions in that block are confirmed and the person who received a payment will now see that his payment is confirmed. So, on one side, the mining keeps the integrity of the coins, and on the other side, it generates more coins into the system.

You can't change any of the transaction IDs without changing the hash. This keeps the whole thing secure.

If you notice that the messages that the sender initiates are not just sent to the address he is sending the coin to, he sends it to all nodes in the network – via the six (or more) nodes he is directly connected to. In just a few seconds that message reverberates across the entire network and all the nodes take note of that message. Once that message is released, and the rest of the nodes bear witness to it, the nodes now deem that the recipient is now the owner of more coins, and that the sender has less.

Let's put this to use in an example.

Let's say Clement wants to pay Bob 1 BTC (BTC = Bitcoin) for whatever reason, which is immaterial to the network. Bob creates a wallet and gets an address. That address belongs to him and it comes with a Private Key. In the meantime, Clement, who already has his address, Private Key, and some Bitcoin in his wallet, takes Bob's address from him and broadcasts a message to the entire network that he is sending Bob 1 BTC. You've already seen how that is then placed in blocks.

Once it is placed in a block, the entire block is hashed, and that is then placed inside the next block and the miner proceeds to solve the puzzle. Once the puzzle is solved, that hash is then placed in the next block of transactions, and so on it goes.

That results in an unbreakable chain. Once the transaction is confirmed, it cannot be canceled or reversed. It lives forever, because a change in even one digit will change the hash, and that change in hash will not jive with the hash that is already recorded in the preceding block.

This blockchain record is kept on all full nodes. That means there are thousands of records of this blockchain, which means it can't be altered.

The fundamentals of Cryptocurrencies in this chapter looked primarily at Bitcoin and to a brief extent, Ethereum. But all cryptos have some form of mechanism that is similar. All of them have the same concept but execute it differently, and by that you get different coins and networks.

The volume of coin demanded and the supply at any given point give rise to a value, and that value is made more fluid and the asset is made more liquid by a vibrant market. Trading in Cryptocurrencies is a three-dimensional proposition. You can trade fiats for cryptos, or you can trade one crypto for another.

BASICS OF TRADING

Trading cryptos is simple. You buy one of many existing Cryptocurrencies that are offered by the exchanges. There are a number of exchanges that exist in the US and in other parts of the world. Before you think about where you want to open an account, here is what you need to consider.

Firstly, you have to set up an account. If you prefer, in any jurisdiction, you will set up an account at a location that will not impose a tax liability on you. So that merits some study. This book won't give you tax advice, but you should be aware that there are jurisdictions that will consider Bitcoin trading profits taxable. If you see it as a commodity and it is not a legitimate sovereign offering, then you are tempted to think it is not taxable. This is wrong. Most tax jurisdictions do not differentiate the underlying asset when accounting for profit. The other thing that people are quick to assume is that Bitcoin transactions are anonymous. Well, they are to a limited extent. But there are easy ways to see who owns what, unless you go through extreme measures to protect it. When people say that Bitcoin is usually used by the shady elements to hide their activities, they don't really know what they are talking about.

EXCHANGES

There are more than a hundred exchanges that you can get on to be able to trade the currencies that we talk about in this book. We will stick to one hundred, and you can look at each one of them to see which ones you would like to pick. You should have at least 10 exchanges in your basket, and you should use the ones that allow you to keep your coins wherever you please and transfer to them only when your trades are open, find an exchange that is quick with withdrawals and an exchange that executes rapidly without the need for brokers. Brokers work against your interests because they cost more and they are unable to carry out rapid trades. Here is a list of exchanges that you can evaluate: Abucoins, ACX, AEX, AidosMarket, alcurEX, Allcoin, Altcoin Trader, Bancor Network, BarterDEX, BCEX, Bibox, BigONE, Binance, Bisq, Bit-Z, Bit2C, Bitbank, BitBay, Bitcoin Indonesia, BitcoinToYou, BitcoinTrade, Bitex, Bitfinex, BitFlip, bitFlyer, Bithumb, Bitinka, BitKonan, Bitlish, BitMarket, Bitmaszyna, Bitonic, Bits Blockchain, Bitsane, BitShares Asset Exchange, Bitso, Bitstamp, Bitstamp (Ripple Gateway), Bittrex, Bittylicious, BL3P, Bleutrade, Braziliex, BTC Markets, BTC Trade UA, BTC-Alpha, BTCC, BtcTrade, BTCTurk, Burst Asset Exchange, BX Thailand, C-CEX, C-Patex, C2CX, CEX, ChaoEX, Cobinhood, Coinbe, Coinbene, CoinCorner, CoinEgg, CoinEx, CoinExchange, CoinFalcon, Coinfloor, Coingi, Coinhouse, Coinlink, CoinMate, Coinnest, Coinone, Coinrail, Coinrate, Coinroom, CoinsBank, Coinsecure, Coinsquare, Coinut, COSS, Counterparty DEX, CryptoBridge, CryptoDerivatives, CryptoMarket, Cryptomate, Cryptopia, Cryptox, DC-Ex,

DDEX, Dgtmarket, DSX, ETHEXIndia, ExcambrioRex, Exchange, Exmo, Exrates, EXX, ezBtc, Fargobase, Fatbtc, Foxbit, FreiExchange, Gate, Gatecoin, Gatehub, GDAX, Gemini, GetBTC, GuldenTrader, Heat Wallet, HitBTC, Huobi, IDAX, IDEX, Independent Reserve, InfinityCoin Exchange, Iquant, ISX, itBit, Koineks, Koinex, Koinim, Korbit, Kraken, Kucoin, Kuna, LakeBTC, Lbank, LEOxChange, Liqui, LiteBit, Livecoin, LocalTrade, Luno, Lykke Exchange, Mercado Bitcoin, Mercatox, Mr, Negocie Coins, Neraex, NIX-E, Nocks, OasisDEX, OEX, OKCoin, OkCoin Intl, OKEx, Omni DEX, OpenLedger DEX, Ore, Paribu, Paymium, Poloniex, QBTC, Qryptos, QuadrigaCX, Quoine, Radar Relay, Rfinex, RightBTC, Rippex, Ripple China, RippleFox, Simex, SouthXchange, Stellar Decentralized Exchange, Stronghold, SurBTC, TCC Exchange, TDAX, The Rock Trading, Tidebit, Tidex, Token Store, TOPBTC, Trade By Trade, Trade Satoshi, TradeOgre, Tripe Dice Exchange, Tux Exchange, Upbit, Vebitcoin, VirtacoinWorld, Waves Decentralized Exchange, WEX, xBTCe, YoBit, Zaif, ZB, Zebpay.

MARKET

If you want to trade cryptos actively, it is not a difficult process once you get your fundamental study and technical study internalized. There are few, if any, regulations on it that you need to abide by, and as long as you do not engage in fraud or theft, and you conduct yourself equitably, you won't need to keep looking over your shoulder.

Remember that cryptos are not physical assets like shares of companies, or fiat currencies that have the legal sovereign banking system – and then further substantiated by other countries, and by the world's banking institutions. Currencies have that, cryptos don't. So that is the first risk that you need to keep way back in your mind. What's the worst that can happen to cryptos? They could be outlawed around the world. The chance of that happening is low, but nonetheless it exists. In our case, that is a good thing because it adds to the push and pull of the market, creating opportunities to buy and sell. It is also one of the reasons you should not keep an open position overnight.

More importantly, unlike shares and currency, they are not physical assets that can be held and kept – cryptos are not physical in any form. These are conceptual assets, and as we advance as a society we will see that cryptos will end up being the most efficient currency in use. Imagine a time when we eventually reach space and have colonies – cryptos would be an ideal way to facilitate commerce.

Up until this point, what we have been looking at has been the ecosystem of the crypto economy – specifically the cryptocurrency. That gives us the basic knowledge to begin understanding the factors we are interested in that come into play for the market. Our next objective is to look to the market. If necessary, I will compare the crypto-market with traditional financial markets.

The first thing you need to know is that there is no clear control of the crypto-market. That means that there are no rules on what you can and can't do yet, but there are limitations on what's acceptable on the market. You can trade manually, you can trading with programs, and you can even use artificial intelligence.

There is no rugulations, and that makes it a very lucrative opportunity if you do three things. The first is make sure you understand the basics. Second, start small-for a few exchanges the minimum trading size is 0.001 bitcoin. You need to get the feeling of how things are going, and that's getting your trust and experience up. The third is you are not stopping at plain vanilla trades. If you just want to get into it and trade one or two times a day with plain vanilla trades, then this is not something that you will succeed at in the way that you imagine. Bottom line: start small and crank it up.

I hear many would-be traders complain that the Bitcoin market is volatile. It is, but that is a good thing. There are two kinds of volatility. One where there is high volume (and the volatility is driven by a different factor) and the other where there is insufficient volume.

TRADABILITY

Bitcoin isn't the only currency you can sell over there. And the USD isn't the only fiat against which you can trade that. Today there are over 1000 cryptos on the market and more than 100 fiats worth trading in. Mastering all these pairings, though, produces a cightmare. You just need to focus on a few. The US Dollar, the Japanese Yen, and the Euro are your best fiats to be exchanged against cryptos, in my opinion. Among the cryptos, apart from Bitcoin, which is the obvious trading option, you can choose from eight alternatives: Ethereum, Litecoin, NEM, Dash, Ripple, Ethereum Classic, Monero, and Zcash.

That brings you over 50 possible trading pairs-USD v BTC, USD v ETH, USD v NEM, etc. Choosing from it might seem like a wide field, but let me tell you that, as a beginner, it is too many indeed. As a manual dealer, knowing, monitoring, and performing each pair's entry and exits will be absolutely overwhelming.

To choose the pairing effectively, you must be intimately acquainted with the nature of the individual currency and the nature of their pairing. To do so you need to analyze and appreciate the essential tradability and liquidity variables.

Tradability is a combination of flexibility and length. Volatility is the amount of change it creates over a given period of time, and width is about the difference between the high and low price movement. You both need to make something economically tradable. Tradability has a lot to do with buying and holding for future profit. That does not include the motions at higher frequencies. On the other hand, if there is no scope, then entering and leaving the market profitably will be challenging, as there are spreads that you need to remember. When you look at a pairing between A and B for example, the exchange rate is 1:1.9. Currently the average is ranged from 1.85 to 1.95. In this example your buy price would be 1.95 and your selling price would be 1.85. If you do an instant entry and exit, this spread would cause you to lose 0,1. The point of highlighting this is to show you that even if the price did not move you would still lose the spread if you entered and exited within moments.

Because of this, breadth of movement is important, especially if you want to do fast trades which can be done by cryptos. You want to be able to have it pass across the spread at least to pay the expenses and other charges, and if that happens, you could pinch the market throughout the day several days and make a tidy profit. We'll dig at that later on.

The way volatility helps is that it gives you a lot of trading opportunities in one day. You have to think about trading as a two-way street, and not as you would if you bought stocks. You are exchanging one currency for another in that two-way street. And so, if you think BTC v ETH fluctuates rapidly, that means the BTC will rise up against ETH and then fall back. When BTC falls back against ETH, that means that the ETH appreciates momentarily. Your hope lies in riding the ups and downs.

If an asset isn't volatile, buying on a long-term basis may be a great asset, but it won't be a good candidate for swift trade or day trade—which is what you want to do with cryptos. When it comes to those things, try not to leave a place immediately. Leaving open positions unattended is too high a possibility-unless you do system trading or using AI.

In comparison to the stock market, the crypto industry is. If they aren't volatile, they don't present a chance for profitability in trade—remember we're talking about trade here. In this discussion, buying an asset for long-term appreciation isn't covered.

On the other hand, they present reduced security and predictability to trade, if they are too volatile. So there has to be a difference in the uncertainty stage. These volatile untenable situations arise by volume. Prices tend to be volatile if the volume is low but they are not tradable. This is because the price fluctuates too quickly to allow market entry to be predictable and then once in, it becomes too difficult to effectively exit the market. The mean volume is a key factor in accepting the asset's volatility pattern. This contributes to liquidity-the second of the two reasons that we have listed.

LIQUIDITY

Liquidity has to do to with volume and efficiency. You can think of it as friction. If you get into an asset, you want it to be as frictionless as possible. That means you get in when you want to and you get out when you want to. There are a few situations that may make that untenable. One scenario that could happen is when everyone wants to sell, you will find that there are no buyers – that's not a liquid market. You may discover that finding a seller or finding a buyer is not easy because there is lackluster interest in the asset; or you may find that there are not enough exchanges supporting the market, which reduces the potential trader's access to that asset. These are just a few ways the asset is illiquid – there are more. But you get the point. When you consider an asset, you need to assess its liquidity and its volatility. Liquidity without volatility does not give you tradability, while volatility without liquidity doesn't give you predictability.

This is partially the reason Bitcoin is more valuable and in demand than its alternatives and the USD-BTC pair is a popular investment tool for day traders. It is also because there is sufficient liquidity to make your trades almost seamless and efficient. This is called a liquidity premium, and it is one that you should be willing to pay, as the payoff is worth it.

But that is a fiat-crypto pair (meaning it is the trade between a fiat currency and a cryptocurrency). What about a crypto-crypto pair? Well, there are several large volume and liquid pairs that you can work with. One such pair is the BTC-ETH pair.

With respect to tradability, you should have your basket well differentiated between fiat-cryptos and crypto-cryptos, and even have a basket that is fiat-crypto-fiat or crypto-fiat-crypto, or some other three-way combination.

You want to be an expert in at least two or three combinations, and that expertise comes in the form of study and practice. You have to study the fundamentals and you have to practice the art of reading the charts. In the trading business these are called the fundamentals and the technical.

You have to study the fundamentals – which includes knowledge of the asset, how it works, market sentiment, regulation, and analysis. On the other hand you have to know how to read the charts. The charts and the analysis of the movement of price is a comprehensive mathematical and statistical representation of the psychology of the market. It is fairly plausible to understand where the market is moving in the future by looking at sufficient data from the past. That's the technical aspect of the analysis.

CRYPTO TRADING

There are two ways in which you can trade in operation. One has a cost advantage so starting with this is good. The second has a professional and accurate advantage but the costs are considerably higher. It is not always a simple choice between one and the other, rather it is a case of increasing from one to the next. Once you start it's best to take the one that gives you the cost-benefit, this is considering you're beginning slowly. If your initial trading exploration is between 5 and 10 Bitcoin, it would not be too obstructive to go online instead. You'd probably be doing between three and five trades per day (24 hours) with this amount. The online exchanges are absolute fine in this case. The online exchanges and brokerage houses provide you with the ability to execute trades, as well as to locate buy and sell points using trading devices. This is something some of the reputable intermediaries have, and most of them are free if you put a certain minimum amount with them.

The other option is for you to stay away from the Bloomberg Terminal online trading platform and get the price feed you need. For most major cryptos, and even some of the more recent ones, Bloomberg now offers real-time quotes. It is incredibly comprehensive. We only had the USD-BTC pair when I first began using it and they have incorporated most of the others over the last few years. They also offer the ability to chart all the cryptos and even give you the flexibility to program directly from your feed your strategy. My current setup pulls the terminal's real-time feed which is then fed into an AI algorithm we've developed.

If you are considering taking this on with some seriousness , then you should not skimp on the supplies you will need. If you decide to follow the Bloomberg Terminal route, go ahead and also get the T1 line. That way, you get super-fast feeds on pricing in real time. When you end up making fast-fire trades, and if you use an online system, even if you have bandwidth, you end up with a lag time that is not acceptable to any degree of serious trading. I had no alternative but to do so online before I went into trading so switched to BT as soon as they started selling it. The speed of the T1 line and the accuracy of the prices allow me to execute quick turnarounds and trade higher volumes in one day and have higher multiple pair frequencies. Ninety percent of my occupations are non-manual, software trades, five percent are AI trades and five percent are manual trades.

When you do program trades, the programs scan for market-wide opportunities at a rate that is considerably more efficient than a human could possibly. Which takes my focus to more trading opportunities, which raises my value and opportunity for income.

TRADING STRATEGIES

There are three trading strategies introduced in this chapter. These strategies will form the foundation of other strategies that you will surely get used to as you mature in your trading abilities. This is assuming that you are new to cryptocurrency trading and have minimal knowledge and understanding of what it is and how to do it. Remember that this market moves constantly.

Hardly a second that goes by when a trade is not being conducted. With more than 50 pairs of currencies and fiats, trading can easily become a full-time occupation.

BUY THE DIPS

Always remember to buy the dips. Dips are moments in the price movement that a march forward is followed by a momentary step back. This is the characteristic of most markets. When you are new to any market, it is an effective way to identify trends. When you are day trading, trends are not what they would be if you were a long-term trader. A long-term trader considers a trend to last anything from a few days to a few months, and enters his position and leaves it for days, weeks, or even months. A scalper in cryptos or a day trader doesn't do that. He actively trades the waves, both up and down, and exits in minutes, or hours, at the most.

Since you are doing rapid trades, you can use the dips to get a better entry point once a mini-rally has started.

This is your first strategy. When you first get started, observe the graphical representation of price movements. Don't look at the numbers, as the numbers can't give you an image of the price as it takes shape. Watch the chart and adjust the timescale to 5 seconds, 10

seconds, and 1 minute to get an idea of the nature of the movement. You will notice that every advance is punctuated by a retracement and every fall is retarded by a momentary uptick. Get used to this patter and use it in your ability to buy the dip.

Never place an order as soon as the market turns from one trend to the next. Wait for the dip, then buy on its next run. That way you can view the rally form rather than face the retracements soon as you get in. It also gives you an opportunity to confirm the push forward. Use the dips as a trigger for your market entry.

Do the same thing when you are shorting the market - wait for the dip. In this case, the dip means that it is backing off its downward trend and momentarily ascending. Wait for it. When it reaches its apex and starts back down, that's when you catch it. Make it a habit to never try to catch it at its peak. Fortune may grant a perfect catch while the price peaks, but it's never a good long-term habit to have.

The apex and the pit have a specific purpose, and that purpose is not for you to harvest or liquidate, but for you to prepare for the next move. Those are your trigger points.

ARBITRAGE

This is an advanced strategy only as far as beginners go, but it is something that you should master right away. Arbitrage doesn't focus on the ups and downs of the market, but rather the mispricing of the market. In cryptos, this is an underutilized strategy, and if nothing else, this is the strategy you should take away from this book. When there are so many pairings, your best bet is to use the automated programs that I use (as described in the earlier part of this chapter). Without automation, you are not going to be able to make use of the greatest benefit that cryptos provide – and that is tradability and volatility.

Back to arbitrage.

In arbitrage, the thing that you are looking for is a mismatch in price between pairs. So, let's say for instance you have the price of A vs B, price of B vs C, and the price of C vs A. If all goes well, and the A:B is 1:2, B:C is 1:3, then it should be that A:C should be priced at 1:6. But in a pricing mismatch, A (in this example) is bidding at 1:6.5. What happens in this case? Look at how simple this is. If I use one unit of A to buy C, I get 6.5 in return. With 6.5, I can use C to

buy B at the rate of 1:3, which will get me 2.167 of B. With 2.167 of B I exchange that back into A to get 1.08 of A. When I first started the arbitrage exercise, I walked in with only 1 unit of A and I exited with 1.08 units of A. This example shows an 8% return. That's not so important, because the numbers are only examples. The point is that this trade would take just 30 seconds to complete.

Now let's look at how you set this up on your trading. Before I forget, there is something that you should do on a daily basis. On any given day, there are numerous mispricing opportunities, and you will not be able to catch all of them manually. You will need a program or an AI algorithm to catch them and execute the trades. Just keep the program running and set it up to either trade automatically, or to seek your approval prior to placing the trade.

If you're not doing this, there are a number of other traders that'll do it. The quickest way to execute this is to get the prize. The guys who deal on web-based websites surely won't be in the race. Therefore, you require extremely low latency networks and real-time data streams to take advantage of this. This can be achieved by your Bloomberg Terminal, even if you are on a T1 track.

ON BALANCE VOLUME

The two strategies you've seen so far are actually enough to get you started, but here's a third one that goes beyond just buying and selling when and if you feel like it. On the top, the logic behind the first is intended to get you to recognise market entry and the reasons for market exit. It's designed to get you familiar with the nature of price movements and the use of charts to visualize them on a deeper level. The second strategy was arbitrage, intended to get you to take advantage of the market's mispricing. That's right on the top. It's built from a broader viewpoint to get you to open your mind to the various ways you can take advantage of the markets.

The last of the three methods is intended to get you to see what the smart money does. By using this technique, you keep an eye on where all the money is going to flock to. If you can get comfortable with the big money movement then you can ride the trends pretty much and scalp the fluctuations.

You need an OBV tracker for doing so. On the Terminal Bloomberg has it pre-installed. Some prominent crypto MT4's also got it. OBV stands for Quantity On Board.

The OBV indicator lets you see how much money flows into any given position.

When you see money pouring into a currency, what happens? You know it's just about to take off. One thing you normally don't see in online or web-based trading platforms is the volume of orders going into the pipeline. What you get when you do that with the OBV is pretty good insight into where the market is going to tip at any given moment.

Conversely, among other things, what you can do is see where the market begins to lose momentum, and either get out of a spot, turn counters, or shorten the asset. How to read the market and what to do get pretty sophisticated once you start getting comfortable with the OBV. But the pending trades and the OBV are the two things you really must keep an eye on.

There's also something called the OBV mismatch, and it's a second-order transaction, in the way that you're no longer only looking at the price of products to assess a deal; you're looking at the impact of the OBV-measured operation around it. When you think there's a difference between two cryptos, then you go to the level they're traded at and decide if the cryptos ' price converges or diverges. If you find them converging, then you should budget for a sell order. When they diverge, then do the reverse.

HOW TO BUY CRYPTOCURRENCY

There are two ways to purchase cryptocurrencies, the first being to use fiat currency (USD, EUR, GBP etc.) to purchase cryptocurrencies through an exchange. Those exchanges work the same way as regular foreign exchanges do. Daily prices fluctuate, and like regular currency exchange markets-they're open 24/7. By charging a small fee for each transaction, these exchanges make their money.

Others charge buyers as well as sellers; others charge a sales fee only. Most of these exchanges would ask you to check your Identification before authorizing you to buy cryptocurrencies for security reasons.

Also note the type of payments each exchange supports. Others require payments by debit / credit card while others only accept transactions through PayPal or bank wire. Below are the three biggest and most trustworthy markets for buying BitCoin, Ethereum and other fiat currency altcoins, such as US dollars, Euros or British Pounds.

COINBASE

Coinbase is currently the world's largest currency exchange and allows users to purchase, sell and store cryptocurrency. Coinbase is arguably the most novice oriented platform for anyone who wants to get involved in the market for cryptocurrencies. Using the platform, once your ID is verified you can use a debit or credit card to purchase cryptocurrency within minutes. Nowadays they allow BitCoin, Ethereum and LiteCoin to be exchanged using fiat currency as a basis. Known for its stellar security procedures and Stored Currency insurance policies. The company also offers a fully functional ios and Android app for on - the-go buying and trading, which is very hClement if you are looking to trade.

KRAKEN

Based in Canada and currently the largest exchange in volume of purchases in Euros, Kraken has the advantage of providing more coin support (also allowing Monero, Ethereum Classic and Dogecoin to be purchased) than Coinbase. This requires margin trading, which will be of benefit to more seasoned traders but beyond the reach of a novice. For other cryptocurrencies such as Dash and Golem, you will need exposure to an exchange enabling cryptocurrency trading.

POLONIEX

Poloniex is the most robust platform on the market, providing more than a hundred separate coins and sophisticated investor data analysis. Low trading fees are another bonus, this is a perfect place to trade into other cryptocurrencies with your Bitcoin or Ethereum.

Poloniex's big drawback is that it does not authorize fiat money deposits, so you'll have to make your initial purchases of Bitcoin or Ethereum on Coinbase or Kraken.

CRYPTOCURRENCY GUIDE

Beyond Bitcoin, there are a vast number of currencies emerging. Some with different characteristics and advantages over Bitcoin itself.

In this section we will examine many different cryptocurrencies and the fundamentals behind them in order to give you the best possible concise information regarding each one. The prices of these coins range from <$1 to over $300 per coin so there's something for everyone here.

One additional note to remember, is that cryptocurrencies are divisible, unlike regular stocks. For example, you cannot buy less than 1 share of Apple stock (currency $159.30). However, you can buy fraction of a

Bitcoin or other cryptocurrencies. Meaning that even if you only have a small amount of cash to invest initially, you can still partake in the market, even if you can't afford an entire coin.

It should be noted that as of August 1 2017, Bitcoin and Bitcoin Cash operate as 2 separate coins. A further in-depth discussion of Bitcoin cash can be found later on in this book.

For each coin I have tried to list all major exchanges that list the coin as a purchasable asset. However, exchanges continue to list additional coins all the time.

THINGS TO CONSIDER BEFORE INVESTING IN CRYPTOCURRENCY

It's not essential to know all the technical details behind a cryptocurrency before investing. However, answering some basic questions will help you decide whether you should invest in a coin or not. Here are some essential questions you should know the answer to before delving into a currency.

- What problem does the coin propose to solve?

- How will the coin solve this problem?

- Why is this coin's solution the best solution out there? Is it the best solution?

- Who is the team behind the coin? What is their development history? How transparent is their code? Is it open source?

- Is there a public figurehead who will take accountability for any issues with development or adoption?

- Does this coin have competitor coins? If so, what is coin A's advantage versus coin B?

Bitcoin (BTC)

The coin that started it all is now one of the world's premiere assets. Sitting at a market cap of over $67 billion, the coin is worth more than global companies such as PayPal. We've already discussed Bitcoin in depth previously, so this section will discuss it for investing purposes. With the price now sitting at a staggering $4,000 per coin, many commentators have claimed that owning Bitcoin is out of reach for the regular investor, but that's a stance I disagree with. First of all, we have to remember that cryptocurrencies are not like regular stocks, in that they are divisible. So if you wanted to invest in Bitcoin, you don't have to purchase an entire coin. You can buy fractions of the coin so even if you only have $100, you can still get started in the cryptocurrency market.

Secondly, Bitcoin's role as a form of "digital gold" continues to make it the world's most valuable cryptocurrency. It also makes Bitcoin ideal to hold as part of your portfolio as many other currencies price movements are linked to it.

Another reason why any portfolio should contain Bitcoin is that if you want to purchase some of the lesser known cryptocurrencies, you will have to do so via exchanging them for Bitcoin as opposed to buying them outright for fiat currency.

Exchanges:

Fiat: Bitfinex, Kraken, Bithumb (ROK) ViaBTC (CN), Bter (CN), Huobi (CN), Bitcoin Indonesia (INR)

BTC: Bittrex, Poloniex, Cryptopia (NZ)

Bitcoin cash emerged as the result of a split or "hard fork" in the Bitcoin technology on August 1st 2017. The end-goal of Bitcoin Cash is to function as a global currency.

The split occured out of problems with Bitcoin's ability to process transactions at a high speed. For example, the Visa network processes around 1,700 transactions per second whereas Bitcoin averages around 7. As the network continues to grow, so do waiting times for transactions. BTCaims to execute further transfers, and to provide lower transaction fees.

One of the main solutions to this problem is to increase each block's capacity, so that more data can be processed at once. This is consistent with addressing the scalability issues that Bitcoin has historically encountered. In the short term, the system itself succeeded, with the first Bitcoin Cash block recording 7,000 transactions relative to Bitcoin's 2,500.

Bitcoin Cash's failure success will depend primarily on Bitcoin's own implementation of SegWit technologies later this year, and the ability to process transactions quicker and function effectively as a currency-rather than as a speculative asset. Detractors have raised Bitcoin Cash security concerns, too.

Most crypto-currency exchanges have widely adopted Bitcoin Cash. There are only a few weeks of data available at the time of writing, so no one has been able to execute BCH as a commodity any long-term trends or technical analysis. The price may well keep rising as further adoption continues. Recent price rises for Bitcoin Cash is largely driven by South Korean demand, with more than 50 per cent of the total volume of trade being seen on South Korean exchanges.

Due to its higher mining ROI compared with Bitcoin, miners were quick to adopt the currency too. The decline in mining difficulties (leading to greater mining rewards) will continue to see miners move their resources from Bitcoin to Bitcoin Cash.

Note: Depending on your exchange, Bitcoin Cash may use the symbol BCC or BCH - double check before executing a trade.

Ethereum (ETH)

Nearly every major exchange will allow buying of Ethereum for both fiat currency and exchange with BTC

If Bitcoin dominated the cryptocurrency space from 2008-2016, 2017 has undoubtedly been Ethereum's year. This relatively new cryptocurrency has made an immediate impact upon the space with some incredible technological innovations that have the potential to be groundbreaking, and game changing.

It is worth noting that Ethereum itself is not a cryptocurrency, it is a blockchain based platform.

However tokens denominated as "ether" are traded on various exchanges. These tokens can be used for making payments on the Ethereum blockchain or exchanged for other cryptocurrencies or fiat cash. Many online articles will use the terms "Ethereum" and "Ether" Interchangeably.

Where Ethereum shines is with a revolutionary technology known as "smart contracts". Dubbed by some as a technology that could potentially replace lawyers and accountants, these contracts are programmable contracts using blockchain technology, that can be set to execute automatically once a certain set of conditions are met. For example, an automatic deposit of 10 ether could be made into person A's wallet, once person A completes a task for person B. Person B has no way of breaking this contract once the conditions are met as the blockchain will enforce the conditions of said contract.

The potential applications for smart contracts are vast. From government, to management, to being able to set up a self-executing will, this is truly remarkable technology. A number of large international banks have already set up think tanks for technology like this, and adoption by any large institution has the potential to send Ethereum's price into the stratosphere. The Blockchain Banking Consortium project involves 43 international banks and aims to create a blockchain network that can enable large scale international fund transfer.

The platform is still in the development stage, and there are to this day, few real world examples of large scale Ethereum blockchain implementation. However, many investors have faith in the technology, which plays a big part in explaining the price rises over the course of 2017. In less than 1 month between May 18 and June 12, the price soared from $96.65 to a peak of $395.03.

Ethereum also suffered from a $4billion single day loss in market cap after a hoax rumor regarding the death of founder Vitalik Buterin gained traction after originating on internet message board 4Chan. Let this example be another warning that cryptocurrencies are more susceptible to market manipulation than traditional assets.

Ripple (XRP)

BTC: Poloniex, Bittrex, Kraken, Coincheck (JP), Bitso (MEX), Coinone (ROK)

The third largest cryptocurrency by market capitalization is one that flies under the radar of most investors and news sources. Launched in 2012 and acting as a payment network and protocol, Ripple aims to enable "secure, near instant and nearly free global financial transactions." Ripple transactions currently process in an average of just 4 seconds. The platform's ultimate goal is to make outdated payment platforms with slow transactions times and high fees like SWIFT or Western Union obsolete.

Many global banking institutions already use Ripple's payment infrastructure, including giants like BBVA,

Bank of America and UBS. For example, using Ripple's payment platform, banks could convert currencies seamlessly, even for obscure countries and currencies such as a conversion of Albanian Lek to Vietnamese Dong. This would also negate the need for intermediary currencies such as US dollars or Euros. According to Ripple themselves, a switch to the platform can save banks an average of $3.76.

With adoption in the global banking sector, Ripple is off to a strong start. Especially if you look at it like you would a traditional start-up.

Ripple also has the largest number of coin tokens (known as XRP) available out of any coin at 100 billion (39 billion available to the public), in contrast Bitcoin only has 16 million and Ethereum 94 million.

Unlike many open source cryptocurrencies, Ripple's source code is privately owned. The 100 billion coin supply was also "instamined", and in theory the owners could generate more at any given time, which would instantly devalue anyone holding coins. The central ownership is also at a clash with those who believe that cryptocurrency should be used as a force against one single owner. Researchers at Purdue University also determined that the platform had "security concerns", although as of writing, there have been no major incidents with the platform.

Dash (DASH)

BTC: Poloniex, Bittrex, Kraken

Short for digital cash, Dash focuses on speed of transaction and anonymity as its 2 main selling points. Previously known as Darkcoin, it was re-branded in order to distance itself from the "dark web" of underground illegal cryptocurrency activity. Dash focuses on privacy, usability and the consumer market. Currently the coin fluctuates between the 5th and 8th largest cryptocurrency by market capitalization.

By speeding up transaction speeds from Bitcoin by using its Masternode network, payments are near instant versus the 10 minute waiting period for Bitcoin transactions. To obtain a masternode, users must deposit a total of 1,000 DASH. This had led to some debate about whether DASH is truly a decentralized currency or not.

Dash is less liquid than Bitcoin, meaning you may have a harder time executing large orders. However, the currency continues to be adopted by more exchanges every month. Dash's growth potential remains determined by its level of accessibility and adoption by the mass market. Once such example of this is BitCart, an Irish based discount gift card website which offers customers up to 20% discounts on Amazon purchases for payment in Dash.

Another interesting area in which Dash is utilized is the recent Venezuelan currency crisis. Venezuelan cryptocurrency exchange CryptoBuyer started selling Dash as just an option to the local Bolivarian currency that was, and still is, hyperinflated. Venezuelans are seeking to protect their savings, and cryptocurrencies like Dash allow them to do this by holding value against the US dollar.

Another area to note is that the richest 10 DASH holders currently hold 10.1% of the total coin value, which is almost double that of Bitcoin and Bitcoin Cash. This could have an impact if one of these major players wanted to influence market movements.

Monero (XMR)

BTC: Poloniex, Bitfinex, Bittrex, Bitsquare

Monero allows users to send and receive funds WITHOUT a public transaction record available on the blockchain. All Monero transactions are private by default. If you believe in privacy first and foremost, then Monero ticks all the boxes. The currency is designed to be fully anonymous and untraceable. This goes as far as their development team, which unlike other coins has no public CEO or figurehead.

Monero also uses "ring signatures", a special type of cryptography to ensure untraceable transactions. This allows users to receive money, without being able to link the address to the sender. This could be looked at as both a positive or negative depending on your viewpoint regarding anonymity. The ring signatures also conceal the transaction amount, in addition to the identity of the buyer and seller. Unlike Dash, Monero has been open source from its inception, so anyone can view the software code for total transparency.

The anonymity of the currency has made it a favorite of the dark web. Before its shutdown, darknet market site AlphaBay had adopted Monero as well as BitCoin to process transactions. Everything from illegal drugs, weaponry and stolen credit cards were traded on the platform. Its anonymity has also made Monero a favorite among ransomware hackers.

It remains to be seen if Monero will branch out to more legitimate use, such as to conceal one's true net worth. Or if it will continue to be the favorite coin of more illicit industries, preventing it from mass adoption versus other coins. This volatility could be used to benefit speculators when they sought to take advantage of the opportunity for mass adoption.

Litecoin (LTC)

BTC: Nearly all exchanges support BTC to LTC transactions

The original altcoin, Litecoin has represented unglamorous yet steady growth in a cryptocurrency scene fueled by hype and large boom/bust cycles. Because of this, many analysts have deemed it the "low risk coin". Announced in 2011 with the intention of being "silver to Bitcoin's gold" and rectifying the shortcomings that Bitcoin faced at the time. Litecoin's coin limit is 4x the amount of Bitcoin's at 84 million coins making it too, a deflationary currency, The time to build a block is 2.5minutes, a quarter of 10 minutes for Bitcoin. Until Ethereum's growth in 2017, Litecoin was the longtime second largest cryptocurrency through market capitalisation.

Because of its block generation speed, Litecoin's ability to handle a larger volume of transactions gives it a big advantage over bitcoin. This means dealers can send and receive payments with zero transaction costs almost instantly. In comparison, bitcoin can take four times the length of time to make the same transaction at a higher cost. Litecoin also has one of cryptocurrency's most active development teams, allowing the coin to undergo regular cutting-edge upgrades such as being the first coin to adopt Segregated Witness (SegWit) technology. This also gives the coin the advantage behind Bitcoin itself of having the second most stable blockchain.

Another advantage for would be investors is the uptake on major exchanges. Nearly all of the biggest cryptocurrency exchanges support Litecoin purchases in fiat currency including Coinbase in March 2017, which was great news for US and EU investors. In terms of market behavior, generally Bitcoin and Litecoin follow a similar pattern in terms of increases and decreases in the currency value. Many investors choose Litecoin as a supplementary option to Bitcoin in order to diversify their portfolio.

For those interesting in mining, Litecoin's algorithm is far simpler which makes the mining costs and barriers to entry lower. Litecoin runs on the Scrypt algorithm whereas Bitcoin runs on the SHA-256. The main significance of this in practical terms is a lower mining cost as Scrypt is less intensive on Graphic Processing Units (GPUs). In 2017, Bitcoin mining is no longer a viable option for the novice or home based miner, whereas Litecoin mining can still turn a profit, even when factoring in electricity costs in first world countries.

Litecoin's detractors have criticized the coin for being "just another Bitcoin with no innovation". The coin was also the victim of a Chinese pump and dump scheme in 2015 when investors accumulated 22% of all the coins in existence before dumping them.

Factom (FCT)

BTC: Poloniex, Bittrex

Like Ethereum, Factom expands on ways to use blockchain technology outside of just currency. While Ethereum is based on two way verification and ensuring contracts are unbreakable. Factom promises to do the same with large blocks of data by providing a record system that cannot be tampered with. This would allow businesses, governments to provide a track record of data without alteration or loss. The practical applications for this include legal applications, company accounts, medical records and even voting systems. Just imagine a world where it was physically impossible to rig an election, or where an accounting scandal like Enron couldn't happen again.

Like other projects utilizing blockchain, Factom cannot be altered because no single person runs the network. The network is collectively owned by millions of users, independently of each other. While data owned by one person is prone to malevolence, hacking, user error and alteration, the same is not possible with data owned by an entire network.

With regards to investing, like Ether is to Ethereum, Factoids are the "currency" of the Factom system. The more applications that are generated using Factom, the more these Factoids are worth.

Factom has already secured a deal with consulting firm iSoftStone to provide blockchain based administration software projects for cities in China. The deal includes plans for auditing and verification services.

Of the technology, Factom CEO Peter Kirby stated "We believe that this will help developers create a whole new class of accountable and tamper-proof business systems. This could be in insurance, financial services, medical records, or real estate – any system where record keeping is essential."

Like other blockchain technology, common questions surrounding Factom are ones of scalability and wider technology adoption. The other main drawback to Factom investing is whether the team can run the system at a consistent profit going forward - or whether the technology will lead to a race to the bottom in terms of price.

Neo (NEO)

BTC: Bittrex, Binance

One of these earliest Chinese based blockchain projects, Neo, formely known as Antshares prides itself on being open source and community driven. The coin has been compared to Ethereum in the sense that it runs smart contracts instead of acting as a simple token like Bitcoin. The project is developed by a Shanghai based company called ONCHAIN.

The Antshares ceo Da Hongfei revealed the rebranding to Neo as well as some projects in the pipeline at a press conference held at Microsoft China Headquarters in Beijing, June 2017. These included working together with China's certificate authorities to chart real-world properties using smart contracts.

Neo's China-based platform provides exclusive access to the world's second largest economy and the largest cryptocurrency sector that could be perceived as a significant advantage relative to other cryptocurrencies. But major disadvantages for the coin itself include a limited number of wallets.

Support and positive press from a global powerhouse like Microsoft can only be a positive for Neo going forward.

Perhaps the biggest determining factor for NEO going forward is support from the Chinese government. While other cryptocurrencies suffer from legal battles with governments, Neo's relationship with the leadership has been low key if somewhat positive, with founder Da Hongfei attending government conferences and seminars on cryptocurrency and blockchain technology. One thing to be wary of with Neo is once again, a Chinese factor. This time it's the language barrier, as much of the news about the coin is published in Chinese originally, there is significant potential for mistranslations in the English speaking world. For example, "partnerships" with Microsoft and Alibaba (China's largest eCommerce company) have been overstated due to poor translations from Chinese news sources. That doesn't mean collaborations like this aren't possible in the future though.

The smart contracts running on Antshares include equities, creditor claims, bills and currencies.

Update as of August 2017: NEO is currently trading at $51.99 - in just a few short weeks the price increased by over 500% .

Golem (GNT)

BTC: Poloniex, Bittrex, Liqui

Golen is a coin token, based on Ethereum blockchain technology. Described by some commentators as the "AirBNB of computing", the value of the coin is centered around the software that can be developed using it.

The founders of the Golem Project refer to it as a "supercomputer", with the ability to interconnect with other computers for various purposes. These include scientific research, data analysis and cryptocurrency mining. For example, if your computer has unused power, using the Golem network, you can rent that power (hence the AirBNB comparison) to someone else who needs it. The user who needs the extra power, has the ability to access supercomputer levels of processing power for a fraction of the cost of actually owning the processing power themselves.

The ability for users to earn money for their unused computing power is, in theory, a no-brainer, however what remains to be seen is the practical application of the technology. The Golem team's lack of marketing visibility also appears to hurt the coins value in recent times. The lack of ability to buy GNT using fiat currency (such as USD) is also a drawback for the mass market.

It should be noted that the technology is still very much in the early development stages and as of August 2017, the team are still looking for alpha testers for the project. The Golem Project has a very real possibility of petering out into nothing. On the flip side - there is tremendous potential for large future gains with the price of a coin still under $0.30.

STEEM (STEEM)

BTC: Poloniex, Bittrex

Steem represents one of the more intriguing cryptocurrencies available on the market today. The currency itself is based on the social media platform Steemit. Users can publish content such as blog posts and long form articles, and this content is rewarded in the form of digital currency. Similar to how Reddit users receive upvotes, Steemit users receive Steem tokens known as Steem Dollars. The financial incentive ensures that users strive to produce quality content. The platform allows posts on a multitude of topics ranging from cryptocurrency discussion, to sports news and even poetry.

Steem dollars are worth the equivalent of $1 at the current exchange rate. They must be converted to Steem in order to exchange to fiat currency or other cryptocurrencies. The rationale behind this is that they can be added to the US dollar rate in order to reduce the risk of inflation devaluing them. Steemit goes further and actually gives users a 10% interest rate on any Steem dollars held in their account for more than a year.

The main drawback is that the success of the coin itself is based on the success of the platform. If the website reaches a plateau in traffic, so will the coin's value. Others have questioned the validity of the site itself, and whether it may be a large scale pump and dump or even a pyramid scheme. The criticism comes from the fact that many of the most upvoted posts were ones that promoted the Steemit platform itself. Concerns have also been raised with automatic posting bots stealing content in order to gain extra voters.

Creators of the site responded to the criticism by saying that there are certain safeguards in place designed to keep content fresh and give users an extra incentive to hold on to their Steem coins. Their method of doing this is with something called Steem Energy. Steem Power is a way people can imprison their coins in the long run by putting them directly into the network itself. Through changing Steem to Steem Support, users have a larger weighting of upvotes on the website and, for lack of a better term, effectively becoming "power users".

One advantage Steem possesses versus other cryptocurrencies is that by design it is the easiest currency to access with zero investment. Instead of simply buying coins on an exchange, or spending money on computer hardware needed to mine coins, users can simply sign up on the website for free and begin posting content in order to gain coins. It represents the lowest barrier to entry for any asset in the cryptocurrency market. Although making significant gains may be tough initially, certain users have made thousands of dollars worth of Steem from just a single post.

IOTA (MIOTA)

BTC: Bitfinex

IOTA, or the rather uninspiringly named Internet of Things (IOT) Coin, is another coin based on blockchain technology, but with a twist.

The team behind IOTA is basing their hopes on a project known as Tangle, which is a technology currently in development that can be described as a blockchain without blocks. In theory, if Tangle does succeed, an entire network can be decentralized. This would lead to ZERO scalability problems that every other coin faces. To be frank, if the technology does indeed work - it could be a complete game changer for the cryptocurrency scene. Imagine a world without unnecessary middlemen, and think of the sheer cost-saving that this would achieve.

The underlying theory behind the coin is near-zero transaction costs, even for transfers of minute amounts of money - something that no other coin or technology promises right now - not even giants like Bitcoin or Ethereum. By focusing on these micro, or nano payments, there are countless uses for both consumer and business based financial technology. The technology is open source, so anyone can see the code behind it, and follow along with the coin's development - if you are so inclined.

The reason for the low price of the coin as it currently stands, is that the technology is right now still firmly theoretical. Issues that plague all cryptocurrency technologies like mass adoption and security will have to be resolved before the coin can take the next step. The development team have many issues to overcome in just the construction of the technology, let alone the marketing.

Dogecoin (DOGE)

BTC: HitBTC, Poloniex, Bittrex

A meme that ended up with actual monetary value. Favored by Shiba Inus worldwide, dogecoin was invented by Jackson Palmer in 2013 and became something of a fad in the cryptocurrency world.

Dogecoin's value largely comes from an internet form of "tipping". The most glaring sample of this is investors donating Dogecoin for posts they liked to Reddit users. Dogecoin eventually became the second most "tipped" cryptocurrency after Bitcoin and the market for Dogecoin exploded to a peak of $60million market cap in early 2014. A campaign to send the Jamaican bobsled team to the Winter Olympics was funded in part by the coin and $25,000 worth was donated to a UK service dog charity.

The coin flamed out almost as quickly as it rose after Dogecoin backed exchange Moolah filed for bankruptcy and CEO Ryan Kennedy aka Alex Green/Ryan Gentle was sentenced to 11 years in prison on sexual assault charges. Kennedy was estimated to have caused $2-4million dollars worth of losses for those who funded the project.

The modern day status of the coin remains that of a lighthearted, enjoyable community-based project that rewards posts from the website. Dogecoin still retains among the most active communities in any cryptocurrency and proponents expect the coin to one day return to its status as one of the internet's most tipped coins.

STORING YOUR CRYPTOCURRENCY

WALLETS & COLD STORAGE

Once you've successfully bought a cryptocurrency, be it Bitcoin, Ethereum or another altcoin, you'll need to store it securely.

Your cryptocurrency wallet is identical to a standard cryptocurrency wallet, in the way that you can use it to spend money, in addition to seeing exactly how much money you have. However, cryptocurrency wallets are different from fiat currency wallets because of the technology behind how coins are generated. As a note, the way the system works means that your money is not stored in a single central place. It's stored in a ledger. It means that there is a public record of possession for each coin, and when a transaction occurs, the record is changed.

You can store your cryptocurrency on the exchange where you bought it like Coinbase or Poloniex, it is advisable not to do this for a number of reasons.

Like any online entity - these exchanges are vulnerable to hacking, no matter how secure they are - or what security measures they take. This happened with the Mt. Gox exchange in June 2011

Your passwords to these exchanges are vulnerable to keyloggers, trojan horses and other computer virus type programs

You could accidentally authorize a login from a malicious service like coinbose.com (example) instead of coinbase.com

Cold storage refers to any system that takes your cryptocurrency offline. These include offline paper wallets, physical bearer items like physical bitcoin or a USB drive. We will examine the pros and cons of each one.

Cryptocurrency wallets have two keys. A public one, and a private one. These are represented by long character strings. For example, a public key could be 02a1633cafcc01ebfb6d78e39f687a1f0995c62fc95f51ea d10a02ee0be551b5dc - or it could be shown as a QR code. Your public key is the address you use to receive cryptocurrency from others. It is perfectly safe to give your public key to anyone. Those who have access to you public key can only deposit money in your account.

On the other hand, your private key is what enables you to send cryptocurrency to others. For every transaction, the recipient's public key, and the sender's private key are used.

It is advisable to have an offline backup of your private key in case of hardware failure, or data theft. If anyone has access to your private key, they can withdraw funds from your account, which leads us to the number one rule of cryptocurrency storage.

The number one rule of Cryptocurrency storage: Never give anyone your private key. Ever.

Paper Wallets:

Paper wallets are simply notes of your private key that are written down on paper. They will often feature QR codes so the sender can quickly scan them to send cryptocurrency.

Pros:

- Cheap

- Your private keys are not stored digitally, and are therefore not subject to cyber-attacks or hardware failures.

Cons:

- Loss of paper due to human error

- Paper is fragile and can degrade quickly in certain environments

- Not easy to spend cryptocurrency quickly if necessary - not useful for everyday transactions

Recommendations:

It is recommended you store your paper wallet in a sealed plastic bag to protect against water or damp conditions. If you are holding cryptocurrency for the long-term, store the paper inside a safe.

Ensure you read and understand the step-by-step instructions before printing any paper wallets.

Bitcoin:

http://bitaddress.org

http://bitcoinpaperwallet.com

Ethereum:

http://myetherwallet.com/

Litecoin:

https://liteaddress.org/

Consult a reputable cryptocurrency forum for the latest recommendations on paper and offline storage wallets.

Hardware Wallets

Hardware wallet refers to items which make up your physical storage private key. The more common form of these encrypted USB sticks.

These wallets use two factor authentication or 2FA to ensure that only the wallet owner can access the data. For example, one factor is the physical USB stick plugged into your computer, and the other would be a 4 digit pin code - much like how you use a debit card to withdraw money from an ATM.

Pros:

• Near impossible to hack - as of the time of writing, there have been ZERO instances of hacked hardware wallets

• Even if your computer is infected with a virus or malware, the wallet cannot be accessed due to 2FA

• The private key never leaves your device or transfers to a computer, so once again, malware or infected computers are not an issue

• Can be carried with you easily if you need to spend your cryptocurrency

• Transactions are easier than with paper wallets

• Can store multiple addresses on one device

• For the gadget lovers among you - they look a lot cooler than a folded piece of paper

Cons:

• More expensive than paper wallets - starting at around $60

• Susceptible to hardware damage, degradation and changes in technology

• Different wallets support different cryptocurrencies

• Trusting the provider to deliver an unused wallet. Using a second hand wallet is a big security breach. Only purchase hardware wallets from official sources.

The Ledger & Trezor wallets are the most common of those. You will build your own encrypted USB wallet for altcoins which are not sponsored by this wallet by following online tutorials.

CRYPTOCURRENCY INVESTING MINDSET

FOMO & FUD - 2 Terms to be Cautious of

In cryptocurrency terms, FOMO and FUD are two of the most potentially dangerous words in an investor's lexicon. No, they aren't the latest hotshot coins coming out of China, they are acronyms that have cost naive traders and investors money.

FOMO - Fear Of Missing Out

This causes people to over invest and throw money at coins without proper research or due diligence. If you spend any time on cryptocurrency forums, you will see hundreds of posts from those new to the market asking for tips on which coins to buy. It seems like every day there is a new shiny object that people are hyping up, causing less experienced investors to blindly throw their money at it. This leads to people buying coins at their peak, and then panic selling them when the coin pulls back a few days later.

The important thing to remember is this, on every investment you make you won't be able to win. You can not buy any single coin at the same time and people are going to make money where you can't. The important thing is to assess yourself and take stock of your own profit / loss sheet. Take a second before engaging in a coin and remind yourself why you choose to do so, then re-examine the coin's assumptions themselves.

Anxiety caused by potentially missing out on huge returns is only natural, and something that nearly all of us suffer from. The best way to combat this is to understand blockchain technology, and to research each coin individually before deciding to invest. By making smart, reasoned investments, you have a much better chance of long term profits.

FUD - Fear, Uncertainty and Doubt

Fear, uncertainty and doubt is anything to dissuades investors from believing in cryptocurrencies and their applications. This can be anything from spreading of misinformation (such as the fake Vitalik Buterin death rumors), to news reports discounting real world usage of cryptocurrency technology.

Certain nefarious cryptocurrency figures have used FUD to push their own agenda while attempting to harm the growth of other coins. This is where it is important to differentiate from reasonable criticism and analysis of a coin vs. FUD. The more informed you are, the easier it is for you to see the difference.

Where you are getting your news from is another factor. Social media is the king of FUD, go to any crypto group on Facebook or watch a YouTube video from one of the larger channels and you will see commentors spreading FUD on every video. Instead, focus on larger crypto news websites where FUD is less prevalent, and remember to consume your news from more than one source.

SHORT TERM GAIN VS. LONG TERM INVESTMENT

Billionaire hedge fund manager and cryptocurrency investor Michael Novogratz made a very good analogy when he compared the current state of the market to the third inning of a baseball game. The market is still evolving tremendously, and there are a variety of short and long-term occurrences that can impact currency prices.

Unlike regular stock market, the cryptocurrency market is running 24/7 365 - there are no delays between information coming to light and the market reacting, there is no dead time.

If you believe in the technology behind the currencies, then these coins absolutely make sense as a long term investment. With many coins, time in the market beats timing the market, which is where our next acronym comes from.

HODL: Hold On (For) Dear Life

A backronym that is a play on "hold" - it focuses on holding on to your coins even when the market is dropping.

A more lighthearted explanation comes from Bitcointalk forum poster "GameKyuubi" who inadvertently invented the term while inebriated (author's note: Do not trade or purchase cryptocurrency under the influence)

With any long term investment, you are going to see market downturns - that's simply how capitalism works. If you panic and sell every time you see a slight dip (and with cryptocurrencies, that's going to happen A LOT), then you've got a surefire way to lose money in the long run.

HODL'ing of course has its potential downsides as well, with more and more coins coming to market - it's obvious that not all of them will continue to go up in price. You can compare it to the regular stock market with blue chip stocks and penny stocks. Just because a penny stock or small market cap cryptocurrency is currently trading for $0.08, does not mean it has the right to rise indefinitely. If the company or people behind the cryptocurrency don't fulfill their promises to the market, then the coin's value will crash and it will eventually become obsolete.

Note- it's easy to see hindsight. And from the other hand, timing of market movements in a market as unpredictable as cryptocurrencies isn't. Carefully approach every investment, and proper research.

Paper profits vs. Actual profits

Remember, until you have sold your coins, any profit you have made is strictly on paper. With the cryptocurrency market being as volatile as it is, profit margins drastically shift and can do so on a daily, or even an hourly basis. That is why I recommend taking intermediate profits for yourself when investing, you do this by sell a proportion of your holdings at a profit.

For example, you buy 1 coin at $100, 1 month later the coin's value has risen to $150. If you trade out $75 worth of the coin at $150, then you still have 0.5 coins worth $75 on paper and an extra $75 in cold, hard cash. Taking money for yourself is a smart play, and something you should absolutely do if you are looking to make consistent profits over time.

The inverse rule of this is to not sell on the dip. If you followed rule number one of investing which was to not invest more than you could afford to lose, you have zero reason to sell at a loss. Yes, you may see scary headlines with "Ethereum drops 40%" or "Litecoin is crashing", but in the long-run, the majority of these coins return to their previous, and even higher levels. If you sell at a loss, then your money is gone forever.

The Chaincoin Pump and Dump Scheme

Why You Should Always Research a Coin Before Buying

The following is a lesson in smart investing, and who you get your information from. Chaincoin (CHC) was a cryptocurrency that underwent a meteoric price rise from $0.05 to over $6 in under a week. Prior to this, the coin was only available on two small cryptocurrency exchanges and had very little total trading volume. The official Github (programming community) and Twitter accounts had been dead for months prior to this, and very few technical milestones had been accomplished.

Despite this, a YouTube channel known as HighOnCoins started heavily promoting the coin. Videos titled "Buy ChainCoin $CHC" appeared on the channel. The channel also encouraged users to set up masternodes (which required 1000 CHC). The channel encouraged people to buy and hold indefinitely rather than trading out for a profit. The underlying theory behind this was that if everyone invested and held the coin, then the price would continue to increase and grow.

However Chaincoin suffered from many fundamental flaws including:

- Lack of differentiation from other coins

- Lack of innovation from developers

- Zero real world applications versus other coins

The initial surge in investing caused a stir in the cryptocurrency community. Mixed reactions ranging from confusion from investors focused on coin fundamentals, to excitement from uninformed players who believed they were part of a get rich quick scheme.

The coin reached an all time high of $6.81 on July 14th 2017, a few days later, developers returned to the coin's GitHub page and made a couple of superficial changes. A few days later the price of the coin crashed back to $1. HighOnCoins claimed this was as a result of hackers, although exchange activity showed a large dumping of coins from a few traders.

Chaincoin currently trades at $0.32.

GitHub blog Store of Value summarized the incident with the following statement "This was a blatant transfer of wealth from the foolish to the nefarious." Let this be a lesson, never invest in a coin based on hype. Instead, do so on fundamentals and belief in the technology.

Conclusion

I hope you have learned many things about cryptocurrency and how you can profit from investing or trading in these coins. There are various factors to consider when investing in coins and you can use these to decide on an investing or trading strategy.

You may want to read this material one or two more times, and make some choices as to what your goals are for your relationship with the cryptocurrency market.

Next, decide how you will go about reaching those goals. Decide on a cryptocurrency exchange and how you will store your assets BEFORE investing in any one or more coins.

Then plan out how much you will invest in each coin. Remember, diversity is important and you should never have all of your long-term holdings in a single coin.

If you're going to buy cryptocurrency, use the average cost of the dollar—that ensures you're not purchasing all of the coins in one deal, instead buying a set amount every month, week or even day across the year. This allows you not to be tied to a single price, but rather to average your investments so that they are less exposed to volatile price moves.

Trade is rational, not emotional. If you're contemplating long-term keeping of money, don't check the charts every few hours, or you'll be going nuts. Things change quickly in this industry so stay informed about news and happenings in cryptocurrencies, you can do that in less than 30 minutes per day. Ensure content is collected from a number of non-biased sources.

AFFILIATE MARKETING

Affiliate marketing is the practice of receiving a fee by selling the goods of other individuals (or the companies). You discover a brand you like, you promote it to others and you earn a piece of profit for every sale you make. Partner promotion is the mechanism through which a partner receives a fee to sell the goods of another individual or business. The distributor actually looks for a product they love, then sells the product and receives a share of the income from each sale they produce. The sales are monitored from one site to another through affiliate links.

HOW DOES AFFILIATE MARKETING WORK?

Since affiliate marketing operates by distributing retail promotion and production obligations through groups, it helps to exploit the talents of a number of people to create a more effective marketing campaign while offering a share of the profit to donors. To do this job, there must be three different parties involved: Wake up at an ungodly hour. Via complete gridlock travel to the school, streets lined with other half-asleep drivers. After mind-numbing chat, grind through email before sweet release at five o'clock.

Sound awful?

What if, instead of struggling with the rat race's monotony and stupor to earn any dollars, you could make money from anywhere at any time— even while you're sleeping?

That is the concept behind the marketing of the affiliates.

It is a popular tactic for driving sales and generating significant revenues online. The new push towards less traditional marketing strategies has paid off immensely helpful for both labels and affiliate marketers. Personally:

• Affiliate marketing power is leveraged by 81% of advertisers and 84% of publishers, a statistic that will continue to rise as affiliate marketing spending increases in the United States each year.

• In the United States, affiliate marketing spending increases by 10.1 per cent each year, meaning that this amount will hit $6.8 billion by 2020.

• Affiliate marketing costs were evaluated at 62 per cent of direct marketing strategies in 2018 yet at the same time attaining three times the push in traditional approaches. In practical terms, 16% of all online purchases can be traced directly to the influence of affiliate marketing.

• Amazon's partner system improved in March 2017, providing producers prices of 1-10 per cent of merchandise sales, allowing affiliates the ability to dramatically increase their passive income on the basis of the channel on which they sell.

• Jason Stone's marketing affiliate, otherwise known as the Millionaire Mentor, was responsible for retail sales as much as $7 million in June and July 2017 alone.

WHAT IS AFFILIATE MARKETING?

Partner promotion is the mechanism through which a partner receives a fee to sell the goods of another individual or business. The distributor actually looks for a product they love, then markets the product and receives a percentage of the income from each sale they produce. The transactions are scanned from one site to another through affiliate links.

HOW DOES AFFILIATE MARKETING WORK?

Since affiliate marketing operates by distributing retail promotion and production obligations through groups, it helps to exploit the talents of a number of people to create a more effective marketing campaign while offering a share of the profit to donors. Three different systems must be required to make this work:

1. Seller, and creators of products.

The distributor is a dealer, manufacturer, company maker, or retailer with a product on the market, whether it is a lone individual or a big enterprise. The packaging can be a physical thing, such as household items, or a service, such as fitness tutorials. Often known as the company, the retailer does not need to be actively involved in the promotion, but they may also be the advertiser and benefit from the share of sales associated with affiliate marketing.

2. The publisher, or associate.

Often known as a retailer, the distributor can either be a person or a corporation selling the seller's goods to potential consumers in an appealing way. In other words, the distributor markets the drug to reassure customers that it is useful or helpful to them, and to encourage them to buy the product. If the customer ends up buying the drug, the partner will earn a portion of the revenue it generates.

Affiliates often have a very specific audience which they are selling to, usually adhering to the desires of that customer. It provides an established niche or personal brand that lets the affiliate draw the most likely customers to act on the promotion.

3. The Customer.

Whether the customer knows it or not they are the generators of affiliate marketing (and their purchases). Affiliates post those items on social media, blogs, and websites with them.

Once buyers buy the product, the retailer splits the income with the partner. The distributor may sometimes choose to be frank with the customer by revealing that they earn compensation for the purchases they make. Some times the customer might be totally unaware of the affiliate marketing system behind their order.

Whichever way, they rarely pay more for the product obtained through affiliate marketing; the retail price includes the affiliate's share of the profit. The consumer completes the purchase process and receives the product as normal, without being affected by the affiliate marketing structure in which they are an important part.

HOW DO AFFILIATE MARKETERS GET PAID?

A quick and cheap way to get money without the hassle of actually selling a product, affiliate marketing has an irresistible appeal to those looking to raise their online earnings. But how does an intermediary get paid when linking the seller to the consumer? The reaction to that is intense. Consumers need not just buy the product to get a kickback from the supplier. The contribution of the partner to the revenue of the retailer will be measured differently depending upon the system. The partner may get paid in different ways:

1. Payable by transaction.

That's the main communications system for affiliates. In this arrangement the retailer charges the affiliate a share of the product's selling price after the consumer buys the product as a result of the marketing strategies of the affiliate. In other words, the partner really must get the buyer to invest in the company before it is paid.

2. Paying for lead.

A more complex system, pay per lead affiliation services makes up for the affiliate depending on lead transfer. The distributor must convince the customer to visit the merchant's website to complete the requested action— whether it fills out a contact form, signs up for a free review, subscribes to a newsletter or installs applications or files.

3. Pay out per click.

This initiative focuses on enabling the licensee to divert customers from its marketing platform to the merchant's website. This means that the affiliate must engage the consumer insofar as they move from the site of the affiliate to the site of the merchant. The affiliate is paid on the basis of web traffic gain.

BITCOIN

Bitcoin is known as the very first decentralized digital currency. They are basically coins that can be sent through the Internet. 2009 was the year Bitcoin was born. The creator's name is unknown; however, the alias Satoshi Nakamoto was given to this person (or persons).

Bitcoin exchange is a new system of money for the internet that works on the concept of digital currency. It initializes the peer to peer payment system for individuals having no central authority; a new concept of cryptocurrency which was initially introduced in 1998. Cryptography controls the creation and transactions of digital money. Bitcoin works through a software system and does not have any central controlling authority so it is equally managed and controlled by its users around the globe.

BITCOIN TRANSACTIONS

Bitcoin transactions are made directly from person to person through the internet. There's no need for a bank or clearinghouse to act as the middle man. Thanks to this, the transaction fees are much lower; they can be used in all the countries around the world. Bitcoin accounts cannot be frozen, prerequisites to open them don't exist, as the same for limits. Every day more merchants are starting to accept them. You can buy anything you want with them.

One can work with the Bitcoin exchange just like it works with any other kind of currency exchange. Just like working with banks, it is easy to make transactions through Bitcoin Exchange. Analogous to physical trade, the user has to pay to purchase Bitcoins. The difference is that the person has to open an account with a Bitcoin Exchanger. The paid asset of the user will be available in the form of digital currency that can be used to purchase any kind of product. Bitcoins can be exchanged with other Bitcoin holders too. This system works similar to the money exchanges in the banks.

Almost in all payment systems, the payments can be reversed after making a transaction through PayPal or credit cards. But with Bitcoin, the situation is changed, as after making a transaction, one cannot get it back or reverse it. So be careful while exchanging your Bitcoins with currency mediums because you may face chargeback issues. It is preferable to make exchanges with other Bitcoin holders near to you.

It's possible to exchange dollars, Euros or other currencies into Bitcoin. You can buy and sell as it were any other country's currency. In order to keep your Bitcoins, you have to store them in something called wallets. These wallets are located on your pc, mobile device or on third party websites. Sending Bitcoins is very simple. It's as simple as sending an email. You can purchase practically anything with Bitcoins.

When doing a Bitcoin transaction, there's no need to provide the real name of the person. Each one of the Bitcoin transactions recorded is what is known as a public log. This log contains only wallet IDs and not people's names. So basically each transaction is private. People can buy and sell things without being tracked.

WHY BITCOINS?

Bitcoin can be used anonymously to buy any kind of merchandise. International payments are extremely easy and very cheap. The reason for this is that Bitcoins are not really tied to any country. They're not subject to any kind of regulation. Small businesses love them because there are no credit card fees involved. There are also individuals who buy Bitcoins just for the purpose of investment, expecting them to raise their value.

WAYS OF ACQUIRING BITCOINS

Buy on an exchange: People are allowed to buy or sell Bitcoins from sites called Bitcoin exchanges. They do this by using their country currencies or any other currency they have or like.

Transfers: Persons can easily send Bitcoins to each other by their mobile phones, computers or by online platforms. It's the same as sending cash in a digital form.

Mining: The network is secured by people called miners. They're rewarded regularly for all newly verified transactions.

These transactions are fully verified and then they are recorded in what's known as a public transparent ledger. These individuals compete to mine these Bitcoins, by using computer hardware to solve difficult math problems. Miners invest a lot of money in hardware.

Nowadays, there's something called cloud mining. By using cloud mining, miners just invest money in third party websites; these sites provide the entire required infrastructure, reducing hardware and energy consumption expenses.

WHERE DO YOU STORE BITCOIN?

Here are a few ways to store your Bitcoins that may be safer than others.

Online Bitcoin wallets

Wallets that can be accessed on the web from any internet connected device.

Desktop Wallet

A desktop wallet offers a number of advantages over an online wallet. While online wallets are easily accessed from anywhere in the world, they are also more vulnerable to potential hacking. Desktop wallets, on the other hand, are accessed only via your private computer, with personal security keys stored just on that machine. Thus, exposure of your security key online is reduced. Nonetheless, desktop wallets are still susceptible to hacks if your machine is infected with malware designed to root out keys and steal Bitcoins.

Hardware Wallet

More secure than a desktop wallet is a hardware wallet. These wallets are bits of hardware, external devices like USB drives which you can carry around on your person. An added benefit of a hardware wallet is the complete anonymity with which you can transact. There is no personal information linked to the hardware, so no identifying data which could be leaked. Hardware wallets are resilient to malware, and if you happen to lose the wallet you'll be able to recover the funds using a seed phrase.

Paper Wallet

A paper wallet is also a relatively safe way of storing Bitcoin, although it requires a bit more advanced understanding of how digital currencies work. Generate a paper wallet online using any number of dedicated websites, or generate the wallet offline for even greater security. Paper wallets are stored easily because they don't take up a great deal of space, and they also offer true anonymity: they are simply a Bitcoin seed written in some way on a piece of paper.

TYPES OF WALLETS

Wallet in the cloud: The advantage of having a wallet in the cloud is that people don't need to install any software on their computers and wait for long syncing processes. The disadvantage is that the cloud may be hacked and people may lose their Bitcoins. Nevertheless, these sites are very secure.

Wallet on the computer: The advantage of having a wallet on the computer is that people keep their

Bitcoins secured from the rest of the internet. The disadvantage is that people may delete them by formatting the computer or because of viruses.

HOW TO SETUP A BITCOIN ACCOUNT

You can acquire a Bitcoin wallet from a Bitcoin broker such as Blockchain. When you open up a wallet through a certified broker, you are given a Bitcoin address which is a series of numbers and letters, similar to an account number for a bank account and a private key which is a series of numbers and letters as well, which serves as your password.

HOW DO YOU SEND BITCOIN?

In order to pay for goods and services or to send Bitcoins to an individual, 3 things are needed. Your Bitcoin address, your private key, and the recipient's Bitcoin address. From that point, through your Bitcoin wallet, you will send three pieces of information, which are: input, balance, and output. Input refers to your address, balance refers to a number of Bitcoins you are going to send and output is the recipient's address.

BENEFITS OF BITCOIN EXCHANGE

No taxation

When you make purchases via dollars, Euros or any other government fiat currency, you have to pay an additional sum of money to the government as tax. Every purchasable item has its own designated tax rate. However, when you're making a purchase through Bitcoin, sales taxes are not added to your purchase. This is deemed as a legal form of tax evasion and is one of the major advantages of being a Bitcoin user.

With zero tax rates, Bitcoin can come in handy especially when purchasing luxury items that are exclusive to a foreign land. Such items, more often than not, are heavily taxed by the government.

Flexible online payments

Bitcoin is an online payment system and just like any other such system, the users of Bitcoin have the luxury of paying for their coins from any corner of the world that has an internet connection. This means that you could be lying on your bed and purchasing coins instead of taking the pain of traveling to a specific bank or store to get your work done.

Moreover, an online payment via Bitcoin does not require you to fill in details about your personal information. Hence, Bitcoin transactions are a lot simpler than those carried out through U.S. Bank accounts and credit cards.

Minimal transaction fees

Fees and exchange costs are a part and parcel of standard wire transfers and international purchases. Bitcoin is not monitored or moderated by any intermediary institution or government agency. Therefore, the costs of transacting are kept very low unlike international transactions made via conventional currencies.

In addition to this, transactions in Bitcoin are not known to be time-consuming since it does not involve the complications of typical authorization requirements and waiting periods.

Concealed user identity

All Bitcoin transactions are discrete, or in other words, Bitcoin gives you the option of user anonymity. Bitcoins are similar to cash only purchases in the sense that your transactions can never be tracked back to you and these purchases are never connected with your personal identity. As a matter of fact, the Bitcoin address that is created for user purchases is never the same for two different transactions. If you want to, you do have the option of voluntarily revealing and publishing your Bitcoin transactions, but in most cases, users keep their identities private.

No outside interventions

One of the greatest advantages of Bitcoin is that it eliminates third party interruptions. This means that governments, banks, and other financial intermediaries have no authority whatsoever to disrupt user transactions or freeze a Bitcoin account. As mentioned before, Bitcoin is based strictly on a peer to peer system. Hence, the users of Bitcoin enjoy greater liberty when making purchases with Bitcoins than they do when using conventional national currencies.

OTHER CRYPTOCURRENCIES

This is a list of cryptocurrencies. There were more than 900 cryptocurrencies available over the internet and growing. By market capitalization, Bitcoin is currently the largest blockchain network, followed by Ethereum,

Bitcoin Cash, Ripple, and Litecoin. Others incluse; Namecoin, PeerCoin, EmerCoin, GridCoin, PrimeCoin, AuroraCoin, BlackCoin, BurstCoin, Coinye, Dash, DigitalNote, MazaCoin, Monero, NEM, Nxt, PotCoin, Synereo AMP, TitCoin, VertCoin, IOTA, SixEleven, Zcash, Bitcoin Cash, BitConnect, Ubiq.

WHAT TO LOOK FOR IN CRYPTOCURRENCIES

Cryptocurrencies use a number of different algorithms and are traded in different ways. Here are the main characteristics that you should consider.

Market capitalization and daily trading volume

A cryptocurrency's market capitalization is the total worth of all coins currently in circulation. A high market capitalization can indicate a high value per coin or simply a lot of available coins. Perhaps more important than market capitalization is daily trading volume: the value of the coins that exchange hands every day. A high daily trading volume relative to the market capitalization indicates a healthy economy with many transactions.

Verification method

One of the major differences between cryptocurrencies is their verification method. The oldest and most common method is called proof of work. To gain the right to verify a transaction, a computer has to expend time and energy solving a difficult math problem. The trouble with this method is that it requires a massive amount of energy to operate. Proof-of-stake systems attempt to solve this problem by letting the users with the largest share of the currency verify the transactions.

These systems require less processing power to operate and claim faster transaction speeds, but concern over security means that few coins use an entirely proof-of-stake-based system.

Retailer acceptance

A cryptocurrency isn't much use if you can't buy anything with it. That's why it's important to know who accepts a currency before you invest in it. A few cryptocurrencies are widely accepted, even boasting partnerships with major retailers. Most, however, have more limited acceptance, and some can only be exchanged for other cryptocurrencies. Some coins simply aren't designed to be exchanged for goods and are built for other purposes.

Cryptocurrencies are an exciting new development in the world of finance. No one is quite sure yet where the technology will lead, but the fact remains that these new currencies offer possibilities that traditional cash can't.

HOW TO BUY BITCOIN

Here are some simple steps to buy Bitcoin

Find a wallet

First of all, you have to find an e-wallet. It is basically a store or a provider that offers software from where Bitcoins can be bought, stored, and traded. You can easily run it on your desktop, laptop, and even smartphones.

Sign up

Next, you have to sign up with e-wallet. You will make an account that will let you store your Bitcoins. The e-wallet trader will offer you a chance to convert your local currency into Bitcoin. Therefore, the more local currency you have, the more Bitcoins you can purchase.

Connect your bank account

After signing up, the trader has to connect his or her bank account with their trading account. For this purpose, some verification steps are to be performed. Once the verifications are performed, then you can start purchasing Bitcoins and get started.

Buying and selling

Once you are done with your first purchase, your bank account will be debited and you will receive the Bitcoins. Selling is done in the same way purchasing is done. Keep in mind that the price of Bitcoin changes from time to time. The e-wallet you are working with will show you the current exchange rate. You should be aware of the rate before you buy or sell.

Mining Bitcoin

There is another way through which you can purchase Bitcoins. This process is known as mining. The mining of Bitcoins is similar to discovering gold from a mine. However, as mining gold is time-consuming and a lot of effort is required, the same is the case with mining Bitcoins.

You have to solve a series of mathematical calculations that are designed by computer algorithms to win Bitcoin.. This is nearly impossible for a newbie. Traders have to open a series of padlocks in order to solve the mathematical calculations. In this procedure, you do not have to involve any kind of money to win Bitcoins, as it is simply brainwork that lets you win Bitcoins for free. The expensive part comes when you start using technology to solve these math problems for you. The miners then have to run software in order to win additional Bitcoins.

HOW TO SELL BITCOIN

Selling Bitcoin isn't quite as straight forward as buying Bitcoin, but fortunately, I'm here to help. When deciding how to sell your Bitcoin, you first need to consider which method best suits your situation: selling Bitcoin online or selling Bitcoin in person. Each option has its own advantages and disadvantages.

Selling Bitcoin online

Selling Bitcoin online is by far the more common way of trading. There are now three ways to go about selling Bitcoin online.

a)   The first way involves a direct trade with another person, an intermediary facilitating the connection.

b)   The second way is through an online exchange, where your trade is with the exchange rather than another individual.

c)   New peer-to-peer trading marketplaces that allow Bitcoin owners to obtain discounted goods with their Bitcoin via others that want to obtain the cryptocurrency with credit/debit cards. The two groups are brought together to solve both problems in a kind of peer-to-peer exchange.

SELLING BITCOIN IN PERSON

Selling Bitcoin in person can, in many ways, be the easiest way to pass on your digital currency. Simply scanning a QR code on another person's phone and accepting cash-in-hand is about as easy as a Bitcoin transaction can get.

If you have friends or family who want to buy Bitcoin, the process is simple. Set them up with a Bitcoin wallet, send them the Bitcoins and collect your cash.

There are several things to be aware of when selling Bitcoin in person.

Agree on a price: Decide on a rate that works for you: Many use a price from a prominent Bitcoin exchange. Some sellers apply a percentage on top of these rates to cover costs and as a convenience/anonymity premium.

You could use a mobile app to calculate prices. It helps to be aware of local fluctuations in price. Price can vary from country to country, often due to difficulties in obtaining Bitcoin with the local national currency. There are many Bitcoin meetups around the world where people are happy to trade Bitcoin and other cryptocurrencies.

Bitcoin is a digital currency that is here to stay for a long time. Ever since it has been introduced, the trading (buying and selling) of Bitcoin has increased and it is on the rise even today. The value of Bitcoin has also increased with its popularity. It is a new type of currency, which many traders are finding attractive just because of its earning potential. At some places, Bitcoins are even being used for purchasing commodities. Many online retailers are accepting Bitcoin for the real time purchases too. There is a lot of scope for Bitcoin in the coming era, and investors seem to be flocking at every chance they can get to purchase a coin here and there.

INVESTING STRATEGIES FOR BITCOIN

This digital rush of money that is sweeping the global investors is not only getting easier, but also riskier everyday. While it was initially a simple peer-to-peer system for small transactions, it is now used for major investments and foreign luxury purchases, which has introduced newer strategies and uses. How does it really work?

Bitcoin is a currency just like any other. It can not only be used to buy and sell, but can be used for investing and sharing, and can even be stolen. While the initial introduction of the technology came with a desktop program, it can now be directly operated through a Smartphone application, which allows you to immediately buy, sell, trade or even cash your Bitcoins for dollars.

Investment with Bitcoins has become very popular, with major sums of money being put in everyday. As a new investor, the rules remain the same as investing with real cash. Do not invest more than you can afford to lose, and do not invest without a goal. Or, as Warren Buffet would say, "Never invest in something you know nothing about". For every trade, keep certain milestones in mind. The 'buy low and sell high' strategy is not as easy implemented as said. A great way to succeed faster when you decide to trade Bitcoins, however, is to learn the technicalities. Like cash investments, there are now several Bitcoin charting tools to record the marketing trends and make predictions to help you make investment decisions. Even as a beginner, learning how to use charting tools and how to read charts can go a long way. A normal chart will usually include the opening price, the closing price, the highest price, the lowest price and the trading range, which are the essentials you need before making any sale or purchase. Other components will give you different information about the market.

Moreover, new investors will often quickly open unprofitable positions. With this, however, remember that you have to pay an interest rate for every 24 hours that the position is kept open, with the exception of the first 24 hours that are free. Therefore, unless you have a sufficient balance to cover the high-interest rate, do not keep any unprofitable position open for more than 24 hours.

While Bitcoin trading still has its drawbacks, like transactions taking too long to complete and no reversing option, it can benefit you greatly with investing, provided that you take small steps in the right direction.

Note: A good investment strategy

If you are interested in Bitcoin as an investment, you might consider following my simple investment strategy:

a)   Buy Bitcoins, and keep them for a relatively long period of time. Resist the temptation to buy more or sell unless you've thought about it very carefully. Just like buy and hold property investing, the long game wins more often than the short game.

b)   If you are a technical expert, you might want to make bets on emerging cryptocurrencies, but only for a short time and only at the beginning. This behavior is more speculation than wise investing. Do it at your own risk.

c)   Do not day trade: Unless you are a professional trader, do not day trade with Bitcoin. Commissions are high, you are probably influenced by something you've just read, and you are defenseless against market manipulation and pump and dump schemes which are still very common.

d)   Have a plan: Bitcoin investors need to have a strategy: It could be trying to pay off student loans, trying to retire, etc. These different strategies will provide a framework to make a risk reward tradeoff decision.

HOW TO MINE BITCOIN

Before you start mining Bitcoin, it's useful to understand what Bitcoin mining really means. Bitcoin mining is legal and is accomplished by running SHA256 double round hash verification processes in order to validate Bitcoin transactions and provide the requisite security for the public ledger of the Bitcoin network. The speed at which you mine Bitcoins is measured in hashes per second.

The Bitcoin network compensates Bitcoin miners for their effort by releasing Bitcoin to those who contribute the needed computational power. This comes in the form of both newly issued Bitcoins and from the transaction fees included in the transactions validated when mining Bitcoins. The more computing power you contribute, the greater your share of the reward.

Of course, there's only one place Bitcoins really come from: MINING. Every Bitcoin you'll ever own, see, or hear about, was at one point mined via the Bitcoin mining network. If you find yourself in possession of a mining rig, go ahead and mine away! Or if you have a computer fast enough to make it worthwhile, that works too.

But be careful! If your computer isn't cooled properly, you run the risk of overheating it, which could potentially break it. Frankly, mining with your computer isn't really worth it. Not anymore. As the mining difficulty increases, it becomes more and more difficult to gain any profit from it. Unless you have a dedicated mining rig, your chance of getting any sort of return from mining is really pretty low.

For Bitcoins, there's an alternative way to hold the necessary records of the transaction history of the entire circulation, and all this is managed via a decentralized manner. The ledger that facilitates the process is known as the "blockchain". The essence of this ledger might require tons of newsprint for appearing regularly at all popular Bitcoin news. Blockchain expands every minute, existing on the machines involved in the huge Bitcoin network. People may question the validity, even authenticity, of these transactions and their recordings into Blockchain.

This too is justified, through the process of Bitcoin mining. Mining enables the creation of new Bitcoin and compiling transactions to the ledger. Mining essentially entails the solving of complex mathematical calculations, and the miners employ immense computing power to solve it. The individual or 'pool' that solves the puzzle, place the subsequent block and wins a reward too. And, how can mining avoid double-spending? Almost every 10 minutes, outstanding transactions are mined into a block. So, any inconsistency or illegitimacy is completely ruled out.

For Bitcoins, mining is not spoken of in a traditional sense of the term. Bitcoins are mined by utilizing cryptography. A hash function termed as "double SHA-256" is employed. But how difficult is it to mine Bitcoins? This can be another query. This depends a lot on the effort and computing power being employed into mining. Another factor worth mentioning is the software protocol. For every block, difficulty entailed in the mining of Bitcoins is adjusted by itself simply to maintain the protocol. In turn, the pace of block generation is kept consistent. A Bitcoin difficulty chart is a perfect measure to demonstrate the mining difficulty over time. The difficulty level adjusts itself to go up or down in a directly proportional manner, depending on the computational power, whether it's being fuelled or taken off. As the number of miner's rise, the percentage of profits deserved by the participants diminishes, everyone ends up with smaller slices of the profits.

MINING BITCOINS

In simple terms, we can define Bitcoin mining as the process of adding transactions to your ledger. The process aids in confirming that enough computational effort is devoted to a block. The process also creates new Bitcoins in each block.

To mine, you should take a look at the transactions in a block and then verify their validity. You should then select the most recent transactions in the header of the most recent block and insert them into the new block as a hash. Before a new block is added to the local blockchain, you have to solve the proof of work problem. This is a problem that is designed to ensure that the new block to be created is difficult and the data used in making the block satisfies the laid down requirements.

Bitcoin uses the Hash cash proof of work; therefore, for you to solve the problem you need to create a hash.

HOW TO CREATE A HASH

If you know how to do it, it's very easy to produce a hash from a collection of Bitcoin blocks. The unfortunate thing is that you can't work out the data by simply looking at the hash - you need to test different blocks.

Hashes are found at the blocks and you have to combine them to prove that your data is legitimate. There are some miners who try to take the easy route by trying to fake a transaction by changing an already stored block.

You should note that each hash is unique and specific to a given block; therefore, when you manipulate a given block, you change the hash. When a given miner runs a hash tag function on the manipulated block, the block is found to be fake, and you won't get any rewards.

MINING REWARD

When you successfully solve a proof of work, you get a mining reward. The number of Bitcoins in the reward depends on a number of factors such as complexity of the problem. For you to make more money you have to solve many problems. You also need to have high-speed computers to enable you to solve as many problems as possible.

Currently, mining pools have sprung up and are founded on a very simple concept. Here a group of miners come together and work on a number of blocks. Once the problem is solved, the miners share the rewards.

HOW TO START BITCOIN MINING

To begin mining Bitcoins, you'll need to acquire Bitcoin mining hardware. In the early days of Bitcoin, it was possible to mine with your computer CPU or high-speed video processor card. Today that's no longer possible.

Custom Bitcoin ASIC chips offer performance up to 100 times the capability of older systems and have come to dominate the Bitcoin mining industry.

Bitcoin mining with anything less will consume more in electricity than you are likely to earn. It's essential to mine Bitcoins with the best Bitcoin mining hardware built specifically for that purpose.

Many companies started making chips that are exclusively used for running the cryptographic algorithms of this process. Antminer is a popular ASIC hardware used for drawing out Bitcoin. Antminer comes with different specifications such as U1 and U2+. Both U1 and U2+ are about the same size. While U1 has a default hash rate of 1.6 GH/s, U2+ has the hash rate of 2.0 GH/s. The process of entering the Bitcoins transactions in the public ledger is known as, wait for it.. Bitcoin mining. They are introduced into the system through this process. The Bitcoin miner can earn transaction fees and subsidy for the newly created coins. ASIC (Application Specific Integrated Circuit) is a microchip specifically designed for this process. When compared to previous technologies, they are faster. The service offered by the Bitcoin miner is based on specified performance. They provide a specific level of production capacity for a set price.

With the right information and tools, Bitcoin mining is not only rewarding, it's also a fun and safe way to transfer money across the internet. To make as much money as possible you need to have the right software and powerful computer hardware.

BITCOIN CLOUD MINING

If you want to invest in Bitcoin mining without the hassle of managing your own hardware, there is an alternative. You can use the cloud to earn your coins. Put very simply, cloud mining means using (generally) shared processing power run from remote data centers. One only needs a home computer for communications, optional local Bitcoin wallets and so on.

However, there are certain risks associated with cloud mining that investors need to understand prior to purchasing.

PROS

Here's why you might want to consider cloud mining:

A quiet, cooler home – no constantly humming fans

No added electricity costs

No equipment to sell when mining ceases to be profitable

No ventilation problems with hot equipment

Reduced chance of being let down by mining equipment suppliers.

CONS

Here's why you might not want to consider cloud mining:

Risk of fraud

Opaque mining operations

Lower profits – the operators have to cover their costs after all

Contractual warnings that mining operations may cease depending on the price of Bitcoin

Lack of control and flexibility.

TYPES OF CLOUD MINING

In general, there are three forms of remote mining available at the moment:

Hosted mining

Lease a mining machine that is hosted by the provider.

Virtually hosted mining

Create a (general purpose) virtual private server and install your own mining software.

Leased hashing power

Lease an amount of hashing power, without having a dedicated physical or virtual computer. (This is, by far, the most popular method of cloud mining.)

BITCOIN AS THE WORLDS CURRENCY

With recent research suggesting that the number of active Bitcoin users is set to approach six million by the end of 2020, the issue of whether the cryptocurrency has the potential to become a global currency is being hotly debated in both the technology and financial worlds.

The key to this currency is that it enables quick and cheap online payments without the need for traditional banking channels. One of the biggest barriers that it has to overcome is the general acceptance of Bitcoin being safe and stable as there is no government regulating it, unlike most currencies. Instead, Bitcoin self-regulates and new coins are issued at the pace at which the miners produce the coins. This is a positive, though, as it is designed to be difficult to create coins so that there is a steady stream of coins being produced.

Bitcoins have been successful in becoming more mainstream with companies such as Microsoft, Dell and Tesla adopting the currency. But transactions are not just limited to bigger companies, with much smaller companies also following suit: you can now order flowers, pizza or coffee with Bitcoins.

As the growth in the adoption of the currency with retailers expands and awareness of the currency increases, so should the confidence in Bitcoin. But there is a large obstacle stopping the currency from becoming mainstream, which is being included in the exchanges. In March 2017, the first proposal for a Bitcoin Exchange Trading Fund was rejected by US regulators, in what could have been a real game changer for Bitcoin but instead saw their currency price fall. With the failure to be accepted by the large institutions, it makes it difficult to see how Bitcoin can grow and become a widely accepted and adopted currency. Further attempts are being made to get Bitcoin listed, which will likely determine its success.

BITCOIN: VEHICLE FOR INTERNATIONAL TRAVEL

The phenomenon of Bitcoins has taken over the financial and business world by storm. In a world where convenience is put at a premium, most people want to deal with something handy and avoid too much hassle. Being a virtual currency, Bitcoins have gradually started replacing the bulky traditional bank notes and cheques. Businesses and banks are conducting awareness campaigns for their customers to take up this mode of payment, as it is stress-free and time-saving. The main advantage is that you can track past transactions and exchange rates on a Bitcoin Chart. The following are further reasons why you should put Bitcoins on your list of must-haves:

Universal

When you are traveling, the process of exchanging currency is quite cumbersome. This is worse when you are going to more than one destination. In addition, carrying large amounts of cash is not only tiresome but also risky. Bitcoins give you the comfort of carrying as much money as you need in a virtual state. It is common among traders all over the world and hence saves you the inconvenience of dealing with more than one currency.

Less costly

When you trade using cash, you are subject to abrupt price changes in essential commodities. You end up spending much more than you had budgeted because of punitive exchange rates. Bitcoins are a global currency that has stable rates and value and will save you the time and high fees.

Secure

Bitcoins are fraud proof due to the heavy cryptography that goes into its making. There are no incidences of hacking or leaking of people's personal information. When you use the conventional money transfer methods abroad, you are likely to fall into the hands of hackers who might infiltrate your bank accounts. With Bitcoin, you alone have access to your account and can authorize any money into and from it.

Irreversible

As a seller, you have probably experienced a situation where a client reverses an already complete transaction. Bitcoin protects you from such incidences, as these transfers cannot be reversed. You should be careful with your Bitcoins, however, as to avoid transferring them to the wrong person.

Convenient

Unlike normal banks that require proof of identification to open an account, Bitcoins allow anyone to access it without asking for proof. Transactions are instant and are not limited by geographical boundaries or time zones, and there is no paperwork involved. To trade Bitcoins, you only need to download the Bitcoin wallet and create an account. You will also never be turned away from opening a Bitcoin account if you are on Chex Systems or owe money to a financial institution.

HOW BUSINESSES CAN BEGIN ACCEPTING BITCOIN

Bitcoins are taking over the crypto-currency marketplace. They're the largest and most well-known digital currency. Many large companies are accepting Bitcoins as a legitimate source of funds, meaning they allow their online products to be bought with Bitcoins. With the extreme facilitation of transfer and earning of Bitcoins, it would be a mistake not to accept these new-found online coins as cash.

Creating your Bitcoin address

First, you will need a Bitcoin wallet. This is the address where customers will send their money, and that process works a lot like email: they input your address (or, more likely, scan your QR code with their smartphones), enter the desired amount and hit "Send."

Like with a cash register, you will probably need to take the money out at the end of the business day and store it somewhere safe. In general, it is good practice to keep only small amounts of Bitcoins on your computer, mobile, or server for everyday use. You may want to store the bulk of your funds in a safer environment. Make sure you use some best practices for securing your business wallet.

Using a payment processor

When introducing Bitcoin to your business, find the best suitable payment processor or the best Bitcoin merchant solution that enables accepting Bitcoins. To make things easy and to protect yourself against the high volatility that affects Bitcoin, find a partner that can manage the process by allowing you to accept Bitcoin payments but instantaneously converting it into FIAT currency. This way, you will be getting your payment in national currency without even having to deal directly with Bitcoin.

Below, you will find a list of some of the most well-known Payment Processors:

BitKassa – Merchant accepting Bitcoin solution,

BitPagos – Bitcoin and Credit Card payment processor

BitPay – Bitcoin payment processor with mobile checkout solution

Bitbay – Bitcoin payment processor with mobile checkout solution

BitPOS – Bitcoin payment processor for online and brick and mortar stores

Coinbase – Offers payment buttons, checkout pages, shopping cart integration, and daily cash out to USD.

Coinify – Bitcoin Web Payments, Mobile Checkout, In-store Bitcoin Payments and Bitcoin Invoicing with recurring billing in Bitcoin.

Coinkite – Full-reserve banking, payment buttons, invoice pages, hardware POS terminals, and Debit-Cards.

GoCoin – International payment gateway and processing platform for Merchants

XBTerminal – Brick-and-mortar hardware POS terminals with payment processing integrations.

Payment processors will charge either a percentage or a monthly fee for their services, but their prices are still far cheaper than what credit card companies or PayPal charge.

Furthermore, payment processors will offer a few applications of their technology: you can send email invoices, set up a POS (useful if you are running a restaurant or cafe, for example) or add a shopping cart plug-in to your online shop.

Finally, if you don't want to hold onto your Bitcoin (say your suppliers and landlord want cash in fiat), these kinds of processors can convert your money into fiat instantly.

Advertise Bitcoin acceptance

It helps a lot to indicate to your customers that you do, in fact, accept Bitcoin. If you have an online storefront, grab a "Bitcoin Accepted Here" banner and paste it on your site, ideally beside your PayPal, MasterCard, Visa and whatever buttons you already have.

If you have a brick-and-mortar establishment, grab similar stickers for your door or cash register here.

Bookkeeping and Taxes

Reach out to your accountant to determine how to keep records of Bitcoin transactions. Some accountancy firms are beginning to emerge that specialize in Bitcoin and other cryptocurrencies. '

WHY SHOULD YOU START ACCEPTING BITCOIN?

The main reasons that drive businesses to integrate Bitcoin as a payment method:

Lower Transaction fees: Bitcoin can reduce credit card processing fees to less than 1%.

No Chargebacks: Bitcoin transactions are irreversible, so it automatically prevents having chargeback's or returns, like what happens with credit cards.

Facilitates International Transfers: Small online retailers and other businesses avoid selling their wares and services internationally because of expensive cross-border transaction fees. Bitcoin relieves the steep cost of international transactions by enabling easier, faster and cheaper cross-border payments.

Fraud Prevention: Bitcoin provides a level of identity-theft protection that credit cards and other banking services are simply not able to offer. Once you receive payment, it will never be disputed.

Faster Payments with less cost: Having funds immediately available is critical for the survival of many small businesses. By accepting Bitcoin payments, you have access to funds immediately, which is available much faster than with credit card payments.

LIST OF COMPANIES WHO ACCEPT BITCOINS AS PAYMENT

Many companies are accepting Bitcoins, many are not. Here is a list of the biggest names who accept Bitcoins as a currency.

WordPress.com – An online company that allows user to create free blogs

Overstock.com – A company that sells big ticket items at lower prices due to overstocking

Subway – Eat Fresh

Microsoft – Users can buy content with Bitcoin on Xbox and Windows Store

Reddit – You can buy premium features there with Bitcoins

Virgin Galactic – Richard Branson Company that includes Virgin Mobile and Virgin Airline

OkCupid – Online dating site

Namecheap – Domain name registrar

CheapAir.com – Travel booking site for airline tickets, car rentals, hotels

Expedia.com – Online travel booking agency

Gift – Buy gift cards using Bitcoin

Newegg.com – Online electronics retailer now uses bitpay to accept Bitcoin as payment

Wikipedia – The Free Encyclopedia with 4 570 000+ articles

Steam – Desktop gaming platform

Alza – Largest Czech online retailer

The Internet Archive – web documentation company

Bitcoin.Travel – a travel site that provides accommodation, apartments, attractions, bars, and beauty salons around the world

Pembury Tavern – A pub in London, England

Old Fitzroy – A pub in Sydney, Australia

The Pink Cow – A diner in Tokyo, Japan

The Pirate Bay – BitTorrent directories

Zynga – Mobile gaming

4Chan.org – For premium services

EZTV – Torrents TV shows provider

Mega.co.nz – The new venture started by the former owner of MegaUpload Kim Dotcom

Lumfile – Free cloud base file server – pay for premium services

Etsy Vendors – 93 of them

PizzaForCoins.com – Domino's Pizza signed up – pay for their pizza with Bitcoins

Whole Foods – Organic food store (by purchasing gift card from Gyft)

Bitcoincoffee.com – Buy your favorite coffee online

Grass Hill Alpacas – A local farm in Haydenville, MA

Jeffersons Store – A street wear clothing store in Bergenfield, N.J

Helen's Pizza – Jersey City, N.J., you can get a slice of pizza for 0.00339 Bitcoin by pointing your phone at a sign next to the cash register

A Class Limousine – Pick you up and drop you off at Newark (N.J.) Airport

Seoclerks.com – Get SEO work done on your site cheap

Mint.com – Mint pulls all your financial accounts into one place. Set a budget, track your goals and do more

Fancy.com – Discover amazing stuff, collect the things you love, buy it all in one place (Source: Fancy)

Bloomberg.com – Online newspaper

Humblebundle.com – Indie game site

BigFishGames.com – Games for PC, Mac and Smartphones (iPhone, Android, Windows)

Suntimes.com – Chicago based online newspaper

San Jose Earthquakes – San Jose California Professional Soccer Team (MLS)

Crowdtilt.com – The fastest and easiest way to pool funds with family and friends (Source: crowdtilt)

Lumfile – Server Company that offers free cloud-based servers

Museum of the Coastal Bend – 2200 East Red River Street, Victoria, Texas 77901, USA

Gap, GameStop and JC Penney – have to use eGifter.com

Etsy Vendors – Original art and Jewelry creations

Fight for the Future – Leading organization finding for Internet freedom

i-Pmart (ipmart.com.my) – A Malaysian online mobile phone and electronic parts retailer

curryupnow.com – A total of 12 restaurants on the list of restaurants accept Bitcoins in San Francisco Bay Area

Dish Network – An American direct-broadcast satellite service provider

The Libertarian Party – United States political party

Yacht-base.com – Croatian yacht charter company

Euro Pacific – A major precious metal dealer

CEX – The trade-in chain has a shop in Glasgow, Scotland that accepts Bitcoin

Straub Auto Repairs – 477 Warburton Ave, Hastings-on-Hudson, NY 10706 – (914) 478-1177

PSP Mollie – Dutch Payment Service

Intuit – an American software company that develops financial and tax preparation software and related services for small businesses, accountants and individuals.

ShopJoy – An Australian online retailer that sells novelty and unique gifts

Lv.net – Las Vegas high-speed internet services

ExpressVPN.com – High speed, ultra secure VPN network

Grooveshark – Online music streaming service based in the United States

Braintree – Well known payments processor

MIT Coop Store – Massachusetts Institute of Technology student bookstore

SimplePay – Nigeria's most popular web and mobile-based wallet service

SFU bookstore – Simon Fraser University in Vancouver, Canada

State Republican Party – First State Republican Party to accept Bitcoin donations

mspinc.com – Respiratory medical equipment supplies store

Shopify.com – An online store that allows anyone to sell their products

Famsa – Mexico's biggest retailer

Naughty America – Adult entertainment provider

Mexico's Universidad de las Américas Puebla – A major university in Mexico

LOT Polish Airlines – A worldwide airline based in Poland

MovieTickets.com – Online movie ticket exchange/retailer

Dream Lover – Online relationship service

Lionsgate Films – The production studio behind titles such as The Hunger Games and The Day After Tomorrow

Rakutan – A Japanese e-commerce giant

Badoo – Online dating network

RE/MAX London – UK-based franchisee of the global real estate network

T-Mobile Poland – T-Mobile's Poland-based mobile phone top-up company

Stripe – san Francisco-based Payments Company

WebJet – Online travel agency

Green Man Gaming – Popular digital game reseller

Save the Children – Global charity organization

NCR Silver – Point of sales systems

One Shot Hotels – Spanish hotel chain

Coupa Café in Palo Alto

PureVPN – VPN provider

That's my face – create action figures

Foodler – North American restaurant delivery company

Amagi Metals – Precious metal furnisher

Amazon – An online company that sells almost anything.

Among others.

LITECOIN

Litecoin (LTC), or cryptocurrency, is a decentralized, open-source payment network. It helps you to receive money, store it and give it to others. It is one of the three main coins, alongside Bitcoin (BTC) and Ethereum (ETC) in turn. Litecoin has been designed to enhance on many of Bitcoin's perceived flaws and to be the silver to the gold of Bitcoin.

HOW ARE LITECOINS MADE?

The way in which Litecoin is rendered is not so different from Bitcoin. Although banks and governments are centralized entities that can literally print money, Litecoin is a digitally created, decentralized currency by its group. Litecoin's code is called a ledger. It functions as a general ledger, tracking every transaction that has been made. "Miners" process these transactions which create new blocks to add to the chain. Thereafter these miners are rewarded with some Litecoin. This acts as an incentive for users to process new blocks and regulates new tokens being created. This process is called job proof where participants are credited for creating new blocks using their own computing power. Where Litecoin varies is in how the job evidence function is measured. Uses SHA-256 in Bitcoin. The trouble with this is that miners can use ASICs to their benefit. An ASIC is a complex piece of hardware meant for a specific task, in this case, cryptocurrency mining. Litecoin's developers were worried that using miner's manipulating the network could lead to ASIC. They had solved using Scrypt. This rendered existing ASIC mining rigs useless and allowed the blockchain to become more democratic in theory. Although ASIC rigs for scrypt are currently available, and AMD graphics cards are up to the task of mining the scrypt algorithm.

REASONS TO INVEST IN LITECOIN

Network effects Invariably, as people first become acquainted with Bitcoin and start learning the ideas of cryptocurrency, they begin to look at what other coins rule the space at some point. Litecoin has become a brand as the' red' of Bitcoin's' gold. Because it's around since 2011, it's a long-standing altcoin that has built up a solid culture, and holds some of Bitcoin's first mover advantage to that end. High Upside As the blockspace of Bitcoin becomes a rare and expensive tool, Litecoin stands to gain by taking up some of the slack that its rising transaction fees experience. Since Bitcoin solidifies as a store of value, many see Litecoin as a possible Bitcoin contender for picking up the slack to serve as a buffer or excess transaction. If Litecoin ends up inheriting this circumstance of use from Bitcoin, the upside potential at such a cheap buy-in should be apparent. Potential interoperability with Bitcoin Litecoin applied SegWit before being imposed on Bitcoin network. The two networks have had several key features on their roadmaps, and both have Lightning Network and Nuclear Swaps. If both implementations are successful, this means that the Bitcoin and Litecoin systems are compliant with low-cost inter-blockchain transfers, ensuring that users of both systems will send payments to each other through chains.

HOW TO BUY LITECOIN

Then, you thought you were going to buy LTC. The next step is to find out how Litecoin should be obtained. The easiest way to earn LTC is through a crypto-currency exchange. You are trading Litecoin fiat currency using those exchanges. Unfortunately the platforms can be difficult to use. You need to take care of that to protect your income. You are pretty much alone when you have any issues. There are two main forms of buying Litecoin.

Which one you want to use largely depends on your tastes. Coinbase If you want to move your fiat currency to Litecoin then Coinbase is one choice. There are several exchanges but the majority of traders would expect Coinbase to be acceptable. This comes with a large range of currency pairs and you might even have the choice of just using your card to buy Litecoin. Coinbase arrives at a decent paiement pace. Paying LTC would typically result in a 3.99 per cent charge for most forms of bank transfers if using a credit or debit card and a 1.49 per cent fee. Upon registration Coinbase requires you to provide your ID and address. This kind of Identity checking is a standard procedure among multiple exchanges. It is intended to avoid using the industry to launder money and other criminal activities. Such verification of the ID would prefer to take another route, specifically because it offers secrecy, to deter traders involved in cryptocurrency traders informed of their safety. LocalBitcoins Instead of directly buying LTC, you should first buy Bitcoin through a peer-to-peer Bitcoin Exchange that doesn't need an ID. One of the best options is LocalBitcoins which allows users to buy Bitcoin with virtually any currency. Once you have the Bitcoins, you'll then be able to trade these for Litecoins at another site. If you decide to use LocalBitcoins make sure you vet other users thoroughly. There is a checklist functionality and you should make sure that you use that function. Some unscrupulous customers have been reportedly cheating new traders. Generally it is best not to do business if you get a bad feeling or see poor reviews. Keep in mind that you'll need to be vigilant about your defense when using an exchange. Always allow the authorisation of two factors and try not to keep all your coins in a single wallet. Also remember never to leave coins in your wallet unless you are planning to trade. The best way to secure your coins is to place them in cold storage or in a wallet for the hardware. It involves keeping the coins in an authenticated wallet that is only available to you. Remember, you have a complete responsibility for your own safety. If you don't own your wallet, it isn't for the tokens. You must also make sure that you keep your wallet open and that you protect your password. For encrypt your device, email, and phone, you'll also need special, secure passwords. Any compromise could lead a hacker's wallet to find its way into your coins. Your own Litecoin doesn't work quickly. You must not only handle the offers but also take extra care to keep the machine secure. You need to be aware of phishing scams, ransomware and other risks. You'll also need to keep a very close list of your wallet access codes. If you lose those your Litecoin investment could end up trapped in a wallet you can't access. A contrast with that added stress is the risks you can not manage. When you're using an exchange, you rely on them to protect you and your Litecoin. The thing is they sometimes struggle to do that correctly. The most notable example is MtGox crash.

WHAT'S THE BEST WAY TO BUY LITECOIN

Our preferred option is not to buy Litecoin at all and instead to use a controlled broker to exchange Contracts for Difference (CFDs). A CFD is a Purchaser-Broker contract. Instead of buying Litecoin directly you'd buy a CFD and take a short or purchase position. You'd either win or lose money depending on the direction the economy is going in. It allows you to make the most of market shifts without ever owning a single Litecoin. There are an eye-watering range of brokers out there and it is very hard to sort the positive out of the bad. The first rule is to ensure the broker will always be a controlled broker. Regulated brokers must meet strict requirements designed to safeguard your assets. You should also look into any bonuses, overnight payments and other resources for managing risk. Brokers normally offer demo available accounts on their online platforms, so you can test the product before you contribute to any one platform.

RIPPLE (XRP)

Originally (and still is) Ripple is a payment processing service that permits global transactions using XRP, its coin. It is a global payment system that was launched in 2012, and as companies embraced it, it has continued to expand, and currency investors have expressed an interest in Ripple.

Ripple uses a Bitcoin-like other cryptocurrenies and blockchain ledger but there have also been technical differences that aim to make transactions easier to process and, more specifically, faster while staying secure..

HOW TO INVEST IN RIPPLE

Ripple isn't "easy" to invest in as we mentioned earlier. There are reports, though, that Coinbase will soon be adding support for Ripple. If that happens, you can probably expect a substantial increase in Ripple's stock, because new investors will easily buy the currency.

However, you have to follow a particular process of buying Ripple.

1. Create A Ripple account. Setting up a Ripple account is the first possible option you have to do. Ripple maintains a list of approved markets which you can access.

Bitsane is a common choice, as it makes transfers from companies like Coinbase to crypto-crypto. It is worth noting that you can not send money to Bitsane (or any other Ripple exchange at present), so you need to go to Coinbase-> Exchange (Bitsane)-> Ripple. So, you're always going to need two accounts: Coinbase / Bitsane Hopefully that will soon change, but that's how it goes today.

2. Buy Ether or btc on Coinbase. You need to buy Bitcoin or Ether on Coinbase when you have a Ripple Account setup on Bitsane.

Once you have a Coinbase account setup it is very simple to do. You just go to the Buy / Sell page and type your info. That Bitcoin will then be inside that account.

3. Move Your Bitcoin to Bitsane You can move it to Bitsane once you have your Bitcoin or Ether on your Coinbase wallet. That's fairly easy to do, too.

Simply click "Balances," then "Wallets" in your Bitsane account and you can see all the different coins that you can hold in your account.

4. Purchase Ripple Once you have your Bitcoin in your Bitsane wallet, you can purchase Ripple (XRP) at long last.

You should press on XRP / BTC (or XRP / ETH) in the top of the Bitsane homepage, and set up an exchange.

ETHEREUM

Ethereum is essentially decentralized software which allows programmers and developers to run any application code. Wait, and what? Ethereum, I thought, was money... Well it looks monetary.

You know, Bitcoin actually uses a technology called blockchain to perform monetary transactions. Ethereum employs blockchain technology to permit applications to be built that can be run in the cloud, can be shielded from abuse and much more (some things get too technical for me here). A bi-product of this, however, is that Ethereum uses a currency to exchange, called Ether, which is like Bitcoin. That is Ethereum's portion of monetary value.

HOW TO INVEST IN ETHEREUM (ETHER)

If you are interested in investing in Ethereum, and Ether in particular, you will need a digital wallet. Ethereum does not transact on any major platform of stocks. You can not go to and buy Ethereum from your online discount broker. You need to convert this into your wallet.

We advise using Coinbase as a digital wallet since it is extremely easy to always use, it also enables you to invest in Litecoin, Bitcoin and it will give you a sign-up bonus.

It's important to keep in mind that Ether (ETH) is a currency, and that investors will regard it as such. You are not buying Ether shares like you'd buy stocks or ETFs. You exchange your dollars for Ether tokens, instead. No dividends, no payouts. The only chance you have is that other individual on the Internet will pay you more for your tokens in the future than you paid them for.

CONCLUSION

In conclusion, we'll be looking at the more positive viewpoints and preferences of cryptocurrency, and considering the additional points that make it a workable elective to more built up forms of money related exchange.

Low Risk of Disruption: The only way anyone can avoid or shut down blockchains is by shutting down the Internet itself, according to David John Grundy, the regional blockchain head of one of the world's biggest banks, Danske Bank. And by now I think you know that's virtually impossible. It's like saying that someone can keep the sun from shining, or blowing the wind.

Portability: Cryptocurrencies can be easily transferred from one wallet to another using internet devices such as laptops, tablets or even smartphones, as opposed to other currencies. You will need to do so with fiat currencies directly or through the same bank. Plus, you don't have to physically carry them with you because they're stored on the Internet. So you can go anywhere with a good internet connection and bring any amount of your cryptocurrencies with you!

Better Value Storage :Only if it is able to maintain relatively unchanged levels of utility or satisfaction over time can you regard an asset as a good value storage. Applying this to financial assets involves having the ability over time to retain the buying power. The ability of a financial asset to maintain value can be estimated through what is termed a fundamental analysis, taking into account both the quantitative and qualitative aspects of such an asset.

The ability to store or maintain value has become the primary basis for investing or holding cryptocurrencies such as Bitcoin, Ethereum, and others. But can cryptocurrencies be genuinely relied on to store money, how can they do it well if they are?

The Gold Connection :Don't be surprised to find that cryptocurrencies are being compared or likened to precious metals, i.e. Bitcoin to gold and Litecoin or Ether to silver while defending the potential of cryptocurrencies to hold long-term interest. One reason-though a shallow one - is the cryptocurrencies colour. Bitcoins are represented visually as gold color whilst Litecoins are represented visually as silver. But there are more than just visual indications that justify believing in the ability of cryptocurrencies to store values like the two most precious metals on Earth. They must not ignore behavioural systems underpinning all types of properties. When more and more people begin to believe that cryptocurrencies such as Bitcoin, Ripple, or Litecoin can hold interest like precious metals such as gold and silver can do, it can help push up the prices of these cryptocurrencies. As their costs increase over time, it is highly possible that they will be able to maintain or reduce their profits within a specific timeframe.

Comparisons with precious metals, e.g. Bitcoins to gold, can be a very strong factor that can influence overall market perspectives regarding the ability of Bitcoin and altcoin to retain or store long-term value. And this can have a huge impact as regards the number of investors who will generally see cryptocurrencies as good investment vehicles.

Small quantity, i.e., deflationary Just like gold in its physical form, usually cryptocurrencies like Bitcoin have a limited quantity of units that are specified or fixed in their respective blockchain protocols. For example, Bitcoin has a cap of just 21 million units which can ever be created. On the other hand, Litecoin has a cap of 84 million units which are also controlled by its operating protocols. That is what makes the long haul of cryptocurrencies deflationary or disinflationary.

Since cryptocurrencies have a finite number of units that are ever to be minted, their stocks are essentially diminishing compared to the amounts of goods and services that they may demand in the future. This ensures it can be expected to increase its purchasing power over the long haul and can have deflationary impacts on goods and services.

Independence from Other Asset: Classes Relative to all other financial asset classes such as commodities or fiat currencies whose prices fluctuate based on the pronouncements or moves made by central bankers or financial regulators, no central monetary authority will control the real value of gold and silver regardless of their macro-political decisions. Because of its sovereignty from any monetary authority, precious metals such as gold and silver can survive price fluctuations over time, which in the long run makes them very good value storages.

Cryptocurrencies are like gold in that they are inherently typically transparent and autonomous.

This means just as gold, government decisions or shifts in legislation have little, if any, direct impact on their long-term principles. The amount of decentralization and autonomy can be a hot topic for discussion among cryptocurrency consumers and developers, some preferring the full version of autonomy while others feel more comfortable with some compromise, i.e. hybrid versions of some form of governance (not from the government) and decentralization. In general, models of cryptocurrency governance can vary greatly with some following a democratic power structure among its consumers when it comes to making major decisions on one end while others go for the authoritarian form of dictatorship on the other. And various other combination or hybrid models are in between. But in addition, cryptocurrencies with more open frameworks can do a great risk in terms of hedging against the possibility of regulators controlling or exploiting their principles.

Underlying or Intrinsic Values: Assets which are considered to be true value storages have underlying characteristics which serve as the basis for their values. These properties, in layman's terms, have inherent utility values, i.e. functional uses that offer them values. For starters, gold is used in the manufacture of jewelry and electronic parts, such as semi-conductors. The underlying value or utility of land or real estate is their ability to have structures built on them, and the amount of foot traffic that their areas receive.

The cryptocurrencies have a lot of potential when it comes to underlying utility value. For fact, for terms of changing the way financial transactions are done online, cryptocurrencies hold a huge promise that requires regulation of contracts, record keeping, and payments. Through the use of cryptocurrencies such as Bitcoin, Litecoin and Ether being embraced in more and more countries, their realistic usefulness prices are growing even more, which can boost their long haul values.

Impossible To Fake :In terms of facilitating online transactions and data or record keeping, blockchain technology is a revolutionary one. Being such, the development of falsified copies of it is practically impossible. And as blockchains continue to evolve, producing useable fake cryptocurrencies becomes even more impossible-if such a term exists.

Impossible to control: Especially for cryptocurrencies whose market capitalizations are already in the billions of dollars like Bitcoin and Ether, one would need a huge amount of money to transact enough units of such cryptocurrencies just to be able to influence or manipulate their prices. For example, if you look at Bitcoin, whose average market capitalization is hovering around US$ 50 billion somewhere, you would need at least US$ 10 billion to play around just to manipulate demand and supply. Even if you're thinking about Ether, whose average market value is much lower at "just" about US$ 25 billion to US$ 30 billion, you'd still need trades worth a couple of billion dollars just to turn markets to its advantage.

Not Exclusively For The Rich: Cryptocurrencies have low entry obstructions not at all like stocks and other budgetary resources that require generally tall sums of trading capitall. This ensures that even those who have only fairly small sums of money to spend will quickly get in. As such, in general, cryptocurrencies have a larger number of investors investing in them to the extent that market manipulation is practically impossible.

Extremely Secure: Ultimately, cryptocurrencies are virtually impossible to steal if you do your research using the correct kind of data, which we'll address later. But in case you abandon them in your exchange account for cryptocurrency this is often the as it were time when it is at tall hazard of being hacked and stolen. So if you follow my advice about storing your Bitcoins or other cryptocurrencies later on, you can make your cryptocurrencies so safe that they'll be virtually impossible to steal.